GIRLPANTS AND GASOLINE

MISSIVES FROM POST-POSTMODERN AMERICA

David E. Zucker

Early versions of several essays within this collection were originally published on the author's website www.SoundADoggyMakes.com.

Earlier versions of "Transformers as an Allegory for Transsexualism in America" and "On Mini-Bikes" appeared on www.GoodMenProject.com. Rights reverted to author. The Good Men Project retains the right to reprint or grant reprint of the original articles in part or in full for promotional purposes.

Cover photo by Jacob Zucker.

This book printed on some percentage of recycled paper. I actually have no idea how much. I'm so, so sorry. If you've paid for it, you've paid with a currency that in some forms is printed on a blend of cotton and other plant fibers, all of which were pretty easily renewable anyway. If you haven't paid for it, please hire me a lawyer so I can sue you.

ISBN 9780991545520 Print
ISBN 978-0-9915455-06 Kindle
ISBN 978-0-9915455-13 ePub

The Sound A Doggy Makes Publishing, Mahopac, New York

10   9   8   7   6   5   4   3   2   1

For Carolyn,

For consistently yelling at me
to be my best.

Contents

GIRLPANTS AND GASOLINE

It's early January in 2006 and I'm standing in what amounts to little more than an abandoned bodega. A crude bar has been erected at the back of the room and a pile of black-and-white replacement floor tiles is stacked waist-high just off to one side of the unlockable unisex bathroom. The window front has been expanded to accommodate a small stage plus a host of lighting equipment and mike rigs. The room's maximum occupancy must be about seventy-five and maybe half as many people have shown up. Including all five bands.

I am in *Club Crannell St.*, which technically *is* located on Crannell Street, though only accessible via Main Street on foot, through two cordoned-off one-way boulevards and apparently some kind of space-time rift in the heart of downtown Poughkeepsie, NY.

All in all, I think I've spent more money on gas driving around trying to find a parking space than I did on the ticket to get in. The club itself is the bottom tier of a three-venue complex including a loft called *The Loft* and a band's biggest chance at local celebrity, *The Chance*. Creative monikers aside, these clubs together form an achievement trifecta for budding pop-punk, Indie, hardcore and metal bands coming out of Northern Westchester County. On Wednesday evenings you are likely to find a group of older gentlemen covering a lot of .38 Special, perhaps even some Joan Jett if one of them is trying (unsuccessfully) to nail an aging, childless rocker-chick who can still squeeze into her leather pants. Next weekend an AC/DC cover band is scheduled, followed by about three weeks of thrash metal. And for some reason Slayer is headlining. Not a tribute band. *Slayer*.

Even with leaflets for Metal Night circulating through the crowd of underage hipsters, I can't immediately put my finger on exactly what causes the palpable air of dishonesty in the room. Screaming girls who look suspiciously like they base their wardrobe choices on MTV original programming are accompanied by some- what effeminate male American Eagle mannequins, who have crammed themselves into the tightest girl pants they could find without losing all feeling below their waists. Ostensibly, this first group is attempting to mate with band members, while the latter group is attempting to improve its chances of mating with the first group.

My reasons for attendance this night are twofold: primarily, I have high-flying dreams of giving the show a witty yet pointed write- up, which I can then try to sell to local papers and ultimately get a job.[1] The more immediate concern is that I have spent the last year working with one band's guitarist, unloading boxes in the back of our local Baby GAP. By Man Law I am obligated to attend at least one of his band's performances.

Rather than look like the Creepy Old Guy better suited to chatting with the club owner and band's families, I have opted to attempt blending into the crowd, arriving well-groomed and wearing a pair of black high-top Converse All-Stars, light jeans with a single strategic hole in the right knee and three t-shirts all layered under- neath a black wool coat. All of these items are designed to accentuate the fact that I weigh approximately one hundred and forty pounds

Girlpants and Gasoline

sopping wet after a buffet dinner.

My outermost shirt was purchased online, merchandise for a webcomic that focuses primarily on young hipsters outside Boston who listen to a lot of Mogwai. Also, there are robots. To refer to the shirt by its online description of "lime green" is almost a disservice to limes, "limons," and 7-Up in general. It is in fact the *exact* color of a ripe lime's peal, batted angrily from atop its perch in a Mexican beer bottle by a member of the IRA leading a Saint Patrick's Day Parade through Boston's South Side. It's also about the same color as a Ninja Turtle.

Outlined in white against this verdant field, in a bold, black script motley with imperfections to mimic a course brush stroke, the word "IRONY" spans the width of the chest. This is my 'Irony Shirt.' I, like everyone else in *Club Crannell St.* tonight, adore irony. It is a basic tenant of Indie culture, in fact, that the more obscure a band is the cooler you are for wearing its merchandise.

Like every band you liked *before* it got big, ironic t-shirts have become unamusing, uncool and–sin of sins–*mainstream*. A hipster's credibility is now in *inverse* proportion to that of one's t-shirt. I've had to interrupt meaningful conversations to apologize and say, "I'm sorry, I didn't mean to stare at your breasts for twenty minutes, but could you turn just slightly to the left so I can find out what your shirt says? It's been bothering me and if I cant't read it I'll never be able to judge you accordingly." Somehow I have been deceived like everyone else in *Club Crannell St.*, into thinking that this is perfectly normal.

The first band, called The Morning Of, comes on late, temporarily adopting another band's drummer and the name "The Choking Tokers" after their regular drummer fails to show up. They jam out two pieces that sound something like an improv session between B.B. King, Jerry Garcia, and three fifths of Blues Traveler, but sensing they are not fully appreciated by the Abercrombie catalog of an audience, they choose to close with an unbelievably accurate note-for-note cover of Rage Against the Machine's "Killing in the Name Of," which rather than offending, actually seems to motivate the crowd. There's something in the sudden juxtaposition that it eats up.

This is when it dawns on me: my Irony Shirt is not actually ironic. It blatantly says "Irony," which is very straight-forward and in itself not at all ironic. Yet everyone *expects* my shirt to be ironic, so any literal statement by a t-shirt aware of its shirtness *becomes* ironic. It could be viewed as performance art if it were hanging outside MoMA in attempt to lure unsuspecting hipsters into an exhibit of postmodern commentary on a culture that has become increasingly postmodern.

Postmodernism in art is loosely thought of as any artwork showing an awareness of the fact that it is art, often expressed through a rejection of the classical values like form or color in previous artistic *-isms*. Think *avant garde*: Andy Warhol and The Velvet Underground. More modern, hip examples might be a t-shirt that reads, "STOP STARING AT MY BOOBS," in tiny, difficult to read print or one of those little welcome mats that says, "Hi, I'm Mat."[2] These items are aware of what they are and how people are normally supposed to interact with them, and by turning these expectations on end take their little jabs at society's preconceptions about shirts and mats and art and whatnots.

However, the Irony Shirt is something of a different animal. It was originally worn by a vaguely hipster-ish character in the internet comic "Questionable Content," by artist Jeph Jacques. The popularity of the shirt amongst readers on the site's forum resulted in a small production of real-world shirts. Continued popularity made the shirt a profitable endeavor and a staple in the comic's online store. Initially only popular among a few die-hard readers, the shirt continues to get noticed and filters out into the rest of society based solely on it's aesthetics and ironic merits. It's the same trend by which indie music

Girlpants and Gasoline

proliferates outward from friends of the band and local listeners to a broader mainstream audience. Basically, shirt is a demo tape.

However there's a more reactionary nature to the "IRONY" design. It is a critique of young hipsters whose shirts have witty slogans, using generalization of artistic design to comment on the *trend* of postmodernism as a fashion statement through the same medium it's mocking. Put simply, it is *aware that it is aware* of being art. It's a kind of triple-entendre, meaning the opposite of what it says while still protesting, however weakly and sarcastically, a tentative earnestness in its literal message. Hipness has driven style and attitude past the realm of 1990s irony and postmodern chic, into what can only be described as "post-postmodernism."

It is a nuanced system of layers. The bright hue of the shirt demands attention, a simple word against the solid field conveys simplicity, an ease of expression. However the font itself is a convoluted, almost gnarled stroke, pock-marked and starkly highlighted, not necessarily worn but *deliberately* imperfect to artificially convey an *aged* and wizened quality. The meaning of the single word is definite, yet in context contradictory, entirely dependent on the reader's level of awareness and his own objectivity. Why you believe this shirt to be amusing is a type of litmus test, designed to weed out the funny, interesting people from a roomful of fashionista poseurs, who are incidentally way cooler and far more popular.

I was once told an almost certainly apocryphal joke about Bob Dylan in which his son, Jakob–himself frontman for rock band The Wallflowers–plays some new material for his father to see what the elder rocker thinks. When his father gave him some notes he did not exactly appreciate–something to the effect of "Turn that crap down!"–Jakob trotted out a teenager standby: "Dad, you just don't *get it!*" to which his father replied, "No. *You* don't get it. *I'm Bob Dylan.*"

Indie is, ultimately, a counter-counter-culture. It's hard to rebel against your parents when you grew up hearing how your parents were stoned on stage, shouting, "Disco sucks!" at Twisted Sister concerts.[3] Thus forms Indie rock, a counter-culture to the counter-culture, hipsters dedicated to sarcasm and mouthing off and giving it all up ten years down the line for a split-level ranch and a minivan. It's about rebelling against parents until they're supportive and then immediately becoming a responsible adult to avoid having such an uncouth image as the aging rocker.

The term "Indie" itself comes from the independent nature of unsigned bands. Where once garage bands, a long-standing tradition in adolescent rock and roll, were either pressed into working hard or simply failing, the advent of MySpace Music, Facebook Groups and cheap, rudimentary recording software, bands not signed to any record label can exist rather easily and with little outside support, producing their own demos and merchandise and booking the odd show here or there. Being a rock and roll god can be a weekend hobby.

Some bands eventually *do* get signed, be it bad luck or latent musical genius, and possibly lose their "Indie cred." This almost certainly requires the band to behave ludicrously hip and annoying, so as to appear only *ironically* successful. Other bands can remain unsigned and are thus Indie and hip without trying very hard to appear as such. Of course they're still irrelevant and unprofitable. Indie bands may *want* to be famous, but they can never outwardly *enjoy* being famous. It can't even look like a possible goal. The best an indie band can openly hope to achieve is *eventually* being famous, just not right now.

It's a logical extension of artists being unappreciated in their own times. If an Indie band can remain unappreciated *now* for sounding different, then there is the slim chance–should its style of music *become* popular years later–that such a band might be heralded as revolutionarily ahead of the curve. It's a gamble, for sure. But if you act like you're too cool, you might be. Retroactively.

Girlpants and Gasoline

It's an incredible gamble trying not to be cool. Ironically, this mentality spreads from the musicians to the audience the same as every other pop-culture phenomenon. The people who like the music congregate together to hear it and end up wearing the same apparel, financially sustaining the same bands and criticizing the same movies with the same jokes for the same reasons. A rough clique forms as malnourished boys and girls vie with each other to prove that not only are they hip and knowledgeable about incredibly obscure bands, but in some far-flung future when a handful of those bands are lauded over all others, they will have the right to say, "Yes, Mommy and Daddy were there. Because Mommy and Daddy used to be *cool*." It's a fight now to be the most actively uncool and independent, so that maybe in the future we'll have the chance to look remotely cool and interesting next to our own legitimately, indisputably cool and interesting parents.

Around 11:30 a band from New Jersey called The High Court arrives on stage. They are the headliners and despite being from out of town, they've brought with them a pretty sizable following of die-hard fangirls. Their lead signer is an affable, clean-shaven young man named J.B. who looks like he still gets carded walking into R-rated movies. He channels an overabundance of youthful energy into exciting and wrangling the crowd. Were the venue a classroom, the owners would likely be calling J.B.'s parents in for a special conference to discuss the possibility of putting their child on some form of A.D.D. medication so as to prevent him from distracting the other children away from the learning process.

As it stands, J.B. is in front of a crowd of identically fashioned non-conformist teenagers, leading a band and utterly reveling in it. "That first band made me want to fuck and smoke weed," he says. As his bandmates' tuning process begins to drag out, he starts assuaging the audience with jokes and stories from the road. He adopts an almost conversational tone in relating how, at a recent gig, a random

David E. Zucker

stranger offered the band drugs, which they kindly accepted. He came backstage after the show, talked about music, rolled two blunts,[4] tucked one behind his ear and simply walked into the ether, leaving the band to smoke alone.

"But that's not the weird part," J.B. says, and the crowd chuckles. "The guy had this giant tattoo on his calf of Lance Bass and he kept going on about it, saying, ' I'm not *gay*, man, I just really appreciate what the guy's *message* is, y'know?'"

J.B. pauses for effect. " So I called him a fag....I mean I've got a tattoo of *Justin Timberlake* on *my* leg." The crowd roars. Apparently gay-bashing is funny, insofar as it is overtly obvious to everyone in attendance that gay bashing is absolutely horrible and at all times funny in no way whatsoever.

"But we don't do drugs," J.B. continues, and at this everybody laughs harder. Even he can't keep a straight face. When he admits that they all do drugs, that High Court drummer, Denny, is probably high *right now*, Denny pauses in toying with his drum kit and can only shrug with bloodshot eyes half-closed and curl his mouth into a sheepish grin. At this J.B. loses his composure completely and bursts out laughing with everyone else.

As everyone recovers and the band shows signs of readiness, J.B. switches to a dower expression and begins orating. "*Fuck* school," he says. "Do *sound*, do *music*, do *drugs*," and the crowd cheers. J.B. is not tall; he's stocky, but with all his gusto he makes being a low-rent rock star look relatively easy. He's willing to work harder if it lets him do what he loves for a living and it shows, which is very probably part of the reason that his band has a record deal.[5] (But only with a small label, of course. At a company you've probably never heard of. He can't risk getting famous, after all.)

In confounding terms, Indie is a triple entendre; it is rebellion through construction of an image of successfully deconstructed rebellion. It separates itself from both mainstream and counter

Girlpants and Gasoline

cultures, juxtaposing both, and this attitude is itself becoming more and more mainstream each year.

Young people in the 1960s fought for the right to say what they wanted to say and to live happy and successful lives. Two decades later yuppies preferred *appearing* happy and successful, generally through cheating, deceit and copious quantities of cocaine. Choosing image over actual substance, yuppies were defined not by what they actually were, but by what they were not. In essence they were the first brand of middle class, sociologically mainstream poseurs.

A full generation farther removed, the old social lies and slight of hand are nothing but par for the course. They're expected. We have become suspicious of anything that even faintly resembles the genuine. We *assume* there is trickery at every turn and so we work *around* it by deconstructing a person's actions in context and extrapolating the true intent. We are a generation of FBI profilers. We are all Clarice Starling, because we are all of us Hannibal Lecter.

We've come to expect less than perfect honestly in life like we look for the twist ending to an M. Knight Shyamalan movie. We look for clues and subtle giveaways in how people around us act, but since we are aware of this we also guard our own behaviors and adjust them accordingly. We scrutinize ourselves, deconstruct our own actions to see how others will perceive us and perhaps alter them in such a way that upon review by others, they will lead only to the conclusions about us we would have others believe. Our lives are akin to a constantly shifting chess game being played out many moves in advance.

It is exactly this kind of commonplace, multi-tiered paranoia that the Irony Shirt criticizes. We have become *aware* that we are aware of what we are, culturally, postmodern and covetous of our ability to look down our noses at artificial meaning. Legitimate, natural significance is less interesting than constructed criticism of other critics. You don't have to *work* for natural meaning. Better to pretend not to notice what we're doing and maintain some semblance of a normal, rebellious image. There is, after all, no hip way of screen printing "MY PARENTS WERE RIGHT" across the front of a black cotton tee. Instead we buy shirts espousing our personal rejectionist attitudes according to irony and aesthetic.

However Irony Shirt rejects this very practice *through* the practice. Irony Shirt denounces denunciation-by-t-shirt by shirt. It openly admits its own absurdity and hypocrisy and would seem utterly hopeless if not for reasserting by its simple presence that it is, still, just a silly t-shirt with words written on it, one I will continue to wear because I support social commentary and because I look damned good in that shirt. That and I'd still hope to attract girls who like irony, skinny men and obscure, unsigned rock bands.

---

[1] In January of 2006, I had absolutely no idea how journalism worked.

[2] Incidentally, the only time this has ever been funny was when one was purchased by my friend Matt, so functioning as a legitimate introduction, a joke, and a social commentary. Also, it functioned as a doormat.

[3] True story.

[4] That's a re-rolled marijuana cigar, for all you parents reading. (You should really stop trying to understand your kids by reading their books while they're out. It is *very* uncool.)

[5] The High Court broke up in June of 2008. Their full-length album *Puppet Strings* is still available from *I Surrender* Records and through Interpunk.com.

KE$HA WOULD LIKE MY BEARD

Biologically speaking, there are six stages in the human life cycle:

1. Prenatal
2. Baby/Infant/Toddler/Cry-Thing
3. Child ("Kid")
4. Adolescent
5. Adult
6. Geriatric/The Aged/Pre-Dead

Each of those has a definable gear-up period, a dominant characteristic for its homeostasis and a definable transition into the next phase. A fetus isn't yet its own separate person (geographically speaking), then it's born and it is suddenly a baby.

Babies aren't real people. For the large part, babies are perhaps half a rung on the human conscious ladder up from a coma patient.

David E. Zucker

They can eat if you put food in their mouths and they can generally manage to keep breathing all on their own. Beyond that, they don't do much of anything, really. They absorb nourishment and expend most of their energy trying to metamorphose into a tiny creature capable of replicating Real Person behaviors. When they can manage to communicate with others and start interacting of their own accord, moving about under their own power, they have gradually managed to become a child.

Now children are basically Tiny Dumb People. They are not technically stupid (yet), merely *uneducated*. Their purpose is to learn the ways of the world such that they will one day be capable of surviving into adulthood and reproducing. They spend most of their time in school or pretending they are already Grownups.

Soon enough, puberty hits and there are teenagers. Adolescence is a bitch but it's a cocoon phase, an apt analogy considering how many times the average teen will vow something to the effect of, "I'm never leaving my room ever again!" Quite fortunately, puberty *does* eventually end and we are left with, at least naturally speaking, a viable adult. The body is not going to grow or distend in weird ways again for a few more decades, eyesight will similarly stabilize and hair will stop growing in places it isn't already needed to retain heat or wick sweat.

Adulthood is the longest period of human homeostasis, wherein one is expected to pass on one's genetics as much as possible until the body starts to fail and, originally, be eaten by a mountain lion. (Or befall some equal tragedy.)

Old Age then, is more the process by which Adulthood transitions into Death, but considering how long it takes and that an individual can have a long, productive existence well after the genitals stop working, it might be best to consider this a separate stage in life development altogether. The ultimate, usually gradual failure of various bodily functions is what inevitably kills the Old As Dirt.

I now propose a *seventh* stage of human development, to be

Girlpants and Gasoline

recognized between the transition to biological adulthood and what would societally be referred to as *functional* adulthood. It's the period where, yes, you *could*–I *suppose*–have children and make a living for yourselves and them, but it'd really be better for everyone in your genetic lineage to just wait, accrue some financial security and a little business acumen before making the by then well-pondered decision to add a twenty-year burden to your own existence.

I was listening to music in the car when Ke$ha came on and asked if I wanted to have a slumber party in her basement. You are *twenty-three* years old, Kesha. And you have millions of dollars, not even including the ones with which you spell your name.[1] Now, I'm twenty-*four*, and I still live in my mother's house, but I'm a poor starving *artiste*. I don't *have* money. I don't even *have* a basement. Granted, I have some very nice things, but they're all crammed into a tiny space I couldn't afford to pay for on my own. I'm a year *older* than Kesha but my endeavors aren't the kind that pay a salary until I've finished and sold them. Ostensibly, Kesha has her *own* basement. In her own *house*. I don't understand why we have to sleep down there. Can't we just boink in her bedroom? I'm sure she has a very nice bed. In fact I'm pretty sure I've seen it in music videos. Granted, she woke up in the bathtub, but the bed I saw looked quite comfortable, especially after a wicked bender.

And that brings me to my very drawn out point: Kesha is a role model (somewhat sadly), and she is younger than I am (entirely sadly). Still, she's societally recognized as a commercially successful[2] person who is, biologically speaking, an adult. Even considering the percentage of her life that is performatively acting irresponsibly, she's still making the conscious choice to be irresponsible.

I'm not saying her's is an invalid lifestyle. Actually, it's a wonderful, hedonistic existence, with few consequences when you get to that level of rich-and-famous. Frankly, it's what everyone our age strives for. And if you succeed? Well, you just netted a boat load

David E. Zucker

of cash for you and your future family, didn't you? It's a low-stakes gamble with tremendous pay-offs for the winners. It's like playing a weekly lotto for meteoric rises in the world of famous douchery.

However, I think we can all agree this is not responsible adult behavior, whether or not it has its own validity and charm. This is why we need a newly recognized stage of human development, with a name that acknowledges the optimistic and idyllic attempts at actively being a beautiful and unique snowflake, before conservative judgment and normality overtake those senses of pride and hope and crush them into a tidy ball of fear of failure.

Since it stopped being acceptable to use the word "retarded" in daily parlance, I suggest we go with that.

---

[1] Aside: Are those *her* dollars? I wonder if she's actually quite poor because every time someone writes her name with the little dollar symbol *she* has to pay for it. At least I hope that's what happens.

[2] She is coming out with her own fragrance. This is very successful and adult-like. She wants it to smell like "blood and semen." This is a very adolescent, untrustworthy understanding of sex. Parents, do not let your daughters smell of blood and semen. If that's what they wear every day, how will you know what they've actually been doing all night?

THE TROUBLE WITH MILEY CYRUS

CELEBRITY AS ARTIFICE

Hannah Montana is about eight different kinds of fucked up, and for once that isn't referring to the celebritant's propensity for substance abuse, public displays of 'twerking,' or paparazzi-induced bouts of upskirts, nipslips, and panty shots. It's more in reference to the fact that Hannah Montana never was a real *person*. Even less so than your typical celebrity, I mean.

Hannah Montana was a persona manufactured by the Disney corporation in 2005, played by a girl named Miley who, in 1992, was born 'Destiny Hope' Cyrus. Cyrus *also* portrayed a fictionalized version of herself, Miley Stewart, who was somehow *also* Hannah Montana. To put this in a context somewhat more accessible to those of us who found ourselves outside Hannah Montana's key demographic, it would be as if Bruce Wayne were still a fictional character, but Christian Bale really spent his nights swinging rooftop to rooftop, beating up petty criminals and instilling fear in the hearts of boom

15

mike operators everywhere. Barring perhaps Andy Kaufman and his Tony Clifton persona, no celebrity has managed to achieve as equal, unified, and *concurrent* success with her own character as Cyrus did with Hannah Montana. Cyrus *was* Miley, who was also Miley, being Hannah.

And yet despite this, Cyrus somehow managed to stay lucid and generally of good mental health throughout her childhood. That actually made her a more attractive, admirable celebrity personality, right up until she started culturally appropriating young urban black culture and cutting her hair like P!nk.[1] With that understanding, there are be five types of grown men in the world:

1. Gay men, who are hereby exempt from the following discussion on the sexual idolatry of child stars;
2. Men born after 1992 who, like Cyrus, are *technically* adults but push the bounds of the term;
3. Boarder-line pedophiles like David Wodderson, Matthew McConaughey's character from the 1993 film *Dazed and Confused*, who would have readily bed Cyrus before she came of age in late 2010;
4. Those who only grudgingly admit now that she is an adult that they would hold sexual congress with Miley Cyrus; and
5. The Delusional.

Let us first discuss the Dave Woddersons of the world. I thought I had seen every depraved, grotesque act the internet had to offer me. I thought I had become completely desensitized to anything not involving open wounds, pre-teens, or animal abuse. Obviously, I had not considered 2010's Bret Michaels/Miley Cyrus duet. It seemed a reasonable thing not to consider, the kind of willfully blind imbecility that sets off mental warning klaxons.

Bret Michaels: diabetic, hemorrhage-prone former frontman of glam-metal band Poison, and bandana-clad, all-around "celebreali-

Girlpants and Gasoline

ty" douchebag. Miley Cyrus: probably the most furiously masturbated over tween idol since Britney Spears shaved her head to look more like Brett Michaels sans-bandana. One is in-and-out of rehab, desperately clinging to any semblance of relevance, while the other was then getting bitched at by TMZ and her father for behaving like a normal college girl at a dorm party. Still, at the height of their popularities both Michaels and Cyrus were hot among teenagers, especially in rural areas. They are both also brunettes pretending to be blondes, and have both been caught on camera doing drugs,[2] so it's not like there were no grounds for a solid partnership. So yes, put the lovely, apparently vulnerable then-seventeen year old on stage with the (r)aging sex (etc.) addict. Brilliant. If I think like a producer I can almost put a reasonable spin on this.

Point the first: Bret Michaels had written a song for his new album "Nothing to Lose," which had backing vocals written for a young, female, country-ish singer, ostensibly to score some of those sweet, sweet genre crossover record sales.

Point the second: Miley Cyrus was at that time a young, female, country-ish singer with a huge fan base.

Quid pro quo: Cyrus scratched Bret's hairy, sore-laden back for the track, and he scratched hers by signing off (and backing her) on a cover of Poison's classic "Every Rose Has Its Thorn" for *her* new album, "Can't Be Tamed."

Result: Cyrus received rock crossover cred while Michaels latched on to social relevance for another few moments, possibly snagging a few thousand more iTunes downloads from Hannah Montana fans wondering who the old guy was with her on stage.

Consequential necessity: cross-promotional awareness requires Michaels and Cyrus appear and likely perform together in a public setting.

This duet was like storing matter and antimatter in the same container, like mixing acids and bases, like … I can't even find dangerous antagonizers more apt to compare. It's like putting *Miley*

David E. Zucker

Cyrus on stage with *Bret Fucking Michaels*. Obviously, the media frenzy following the debacle had to maintain a double standard completely disparate of any logical claim one might have had against the performance. Controversy erupted over Cyrus appearing on Michaels' track because its lyrics were considered somewhat *racy* for a young girl to sing alongside a grown man. *This* we had a problem with? Seventeen is old enough to have legally knocked Michaels' boots in thirty-eight states, most of which lie in both their key demographics, and we will actively place her in the position where such seems a not unrealistic possibility, but heaven forbid we let a former teenybopper branch out into musical maturity. When it's collaborative, *shame*, but put her in close proximity to a walking STI in order to sell *her* album? No problem there, so long as we never acknowledge it was a sales strategy.

We've constructed a pure, virginal character and expect a young girl to maintain that role ~~for the rest of her life~~ until she implodes after reaching adulthood and thus passing her point of maximum relevance. The next time you're in a music store,[3] act casual and take a look at the cover of "Can't Be Tamed" when no one is looking. It looks like bad Jessica Alba *Dark Angel* cosplay. Cyrus is all made up with sexy bed hair and a studded leather, her bare midriff firmly toned and tanned and likely airbrushed to all hell. She does not look like the type of girl who dates a Jo-Bro of a Hemsworth. She looks like the type of girl who would crack a Jo-Bro over the head with a pool cue and call him an epithet, then bang Bret Michaels.

Bret Michaels is a scumbag. We've known this since 1983. The rules with him are the same as going to the zoo: don't feed the Bret. Don't get too close to the Bret. Don't complain when you throw your sinewy teenage pop stars into the Bret's cage and they get eaten up/out.

Now I am certainly a delusional man. I profess to loath Miley

Girlpants and Gasoline

Cyrus, but this belies a core belief I've secretly harbored for a while now: I really just think Miley Cyrus would like me better than you.

Let me be clear: I do not like Miley Cyrus. At all, really. It's nothing personal, no slight against her. I'm sure Ms. Cyrus is a very sweet, nice person. She just happens to embody essentially everything I hate about Pop Music culture:

- She was a manufactured celebrity.
- Her vocal talent is electronically augmented, which overshadows the (already weak) musical content of songs written for her *by other artists*.
- She was encouraged to remain pure and unblemished in the public eye for the full run of her celebrity, essentially making her seem even less genuine and aware of who she is and making even the slightest action outside this image shocking.
- She became a paragon of success for the business model of eroticizing adolescence.

That, and between chipmunk cheeks and the half of her accent that survived voice coaching, I've found her a little hard to understand since I lost a little of my low-end hearing, but that's not something I can really fault her for; it's my cross to bear for years of listening to louder, better music.

Yet herein lies a paradox: as much as I loath her on principle, I have to admit that under the weird finding-myself fashion blitz and attempts to replicate Lady Gaga's taste for nude performance art, Miley Cyrus is probably not a terrible person, nor is she aesthetically unattractive, nor uninteresting. I hate to think the corporate-funded image consultations and the hype machine actually affected me, but it's either that or I must actively like her music, which is most certainly not the case. As much as I hate pop and country, I'll grant that both can be catchy. As much as I hate processed vocals and that wavering, arpegiated glissando crap overused by lousy singers who can't hold a steady note, that makes them sound passable. Sometimes, from an aurally aesthetic standpoint, it can even sound *good*.

In my defense, none of this has anything at all to do with the person born Destiny Hope Cyrus. They are, for all purposes, super-fluous to any discussion of why I should dislike *her*, and that's the precise problem. *Philosophically*, if I were to hate Miley Cyrus for her commercial image (Hannah or otherwise)[4], I would be putting more value in that than who she is as an actual *person*, and that would make me no better than the executive board at Disney Studios.©®™

In 2011, the first year she was eligible, Cyrus was ranked number 64 on the Maxim Hot 100 list.[5] Two years later she was Number 1.[6] Aesthetically, Miley Cyrus is a pretty lady. She seems to care about family and children and disaster victims and maintaining a healthy lifestyle. She apparently digs some '80s rock and is open to trying mind-enhancing substances as long as they are legal and she is of age in the country she openly procures them. If she enjoys it, she is apparently not averse to shaking her bum. Were I to meet Ms. Cyrus–in a crowded New York City coffee shop, perhaps–and she were to not be in Star Mode–say at the tail end of a 15 minute respite from personal assistants and in dire need of a ¾-caf latte with extra foam and a hazelnut biscotto–I would be forced to treat her like a normal human being. A not unattractive human, sure, but what leeway granted her would be tempered by my distaste for the public image she willfully cultivates.

I would be cool, possibly even cold, incapable of becoming starstruck. This, sadly, would only endear me to her, while my own natural wit and dry humor would seal the deal as I charmingly force her to wait her turn to be served in line behind me. By a method I cannot fathom now but which would be readily apparent in the moment this happens, I would manage to silently have her order

Girlpants and Gasoline

tagged onto my own–possibly through a close friendship with the barista–such that as I left, Cyrus would find her order waiting and ready to diffuse the anger brought her by my gruff treatment. I would then exit the cafe with an amazing story, looking awesome.

This situation of course assumes that I:

a. develop a taste for coffee, and
b. move to a major city where I frequent a coffee shoppe conveniently located near major media centers.

A problem derives from the obvious result that Miley Cyrus would become hopelessly enamored with me and my anti-elitist ways, using her nearly unlimited resources to track me down and the both of us would experience wacky hijinks as we co-star in the worst romantic comedy since Kelly Clarkson starred in that one beach movie with the guy who lost to Kelly Clarkson. This is a "problem" insofar as I could only treat Cyrus like an actual human being, when in fact she has taken great pains to ensure I consider her only as a caricatured creation, this ethereal being of glitter and teddybear stuffing. Also, that image makes me want to throw up a little.

There is no situation in which I could behave differently after randomly bumping into a former teen pop star, because I'm–I like to think–a decent human being. Yes, I rant and rave in my head when motorists don't signal, but I calm myself, I consider their lives, and I forgive. They're real people too, and real people generally try their best or at least choose to do what they think will be to their greatest benefit. No one ever tries to be *evil*, and no one will ever knowingly endanger or hinder themselves. Everything they do is done to maintain or advance themselves, and that's something with which it's easy to sympathize. So then what if the icon with which I'm sympathizing isn't real?

David E. Zucker

Miley Cyrus is Unreal, but in a period where Realness is antithetical to image, and image is everything. Cindy Crawford's mole, as a concept, has been completely supplanted by both Photoshop *and* the collective knowledge and acceptance of Photoshop's constant, often imperceptible alterations to our expectations. While digital artistry makes real life less necessary to visual media[7], *actual* celebrities are being supplanted by *artificial* ones.[8]

Virtual groups have long existed as a concept, though most in a novel capacity, Alvin and the Chipmunks and The Monkees being two of the most successful examples. Whether cartoon(ish) or live(-ish), fans were aware that these groups were *fictitious*, at least at their outset. Paula Abdul dancing with M.C. Skat Cat in 1989's "Opposites Attract" was clearly a gimmick, likely influenced by the previous year's box office success *Who Framed Roger Rabbit?*. It seems *unreasonable* to believe she interacted with an anthropomorphic cat anymore than Bob Hoskins did a rabbit or Dick van Dyke danced with Mary Poppins' penguins.

Something odd changed in 2006, though. At the live broadcast of the Grammy Awards, Madonna got on stage and did a set with fictional band Gorillaz. There was something of a stir when it was announced cartoon characters would be performing live, on stage, and the word "hologram" was getting thrown around a lot, but when the lights came up, there were simply cartoons playing their instruments and singing on stage. They showboated, checked their cell phones, breathed, tripped over chairs, and were generally very lifelike for projected images. Some people came out and rapped in front of the stage, stood next to the figures, and did the Bob Hoskins thing.

Then the thing happened: Madonna came out as they began to perform a mashup of "Feel Good Inc." And her own "Hung UP," and she passed *behind* the projections. The hope had been to be impressed that a cartoon and a live performer wouldn't look completely ridiculous live on stage, not that they could interact in 3D space

Girlpants and Gasoline

believably. Even those who had guessed at the fundamental mechanics of the trick[9] were shocked by not only the execution, but the audacity that it was even attempted. While clearly unreal, by so drastically exceeding expectations, the project forced audiences to suspend their disbelief and accept that what they witnessed had corporeal form, if only because they couldn't process it properly as it was happening.

Soon long-dead celebrities, predominantly rappers and briefly very much not-dead 2008 presidential election CNN correspondent Jessica Yellin, were appearing in-concert and live before audiences in capacities that were just not *possible*, yet were Real. A digital recreation of Tupac Shakur famously 'performed' at Coachella 2012 with Dr. Dre and Snoop Lion, née Dog. Once the technology for this became easily replicable—much like pop stars in general—it only took a few years before the genesis of the first 100% artificial celebrities.

Taking a page from the critically mediocre Al Pacino vehicle *S1m0ne*, in which a director becomes trapped in his own lie after replacing a prima donna actress with an all-digital starlet, Japanese sweets company Ezaki Glico admitted in 2011 to having created for their promotional campaign a new "member" of multitudinous girl group AKB48. "Miss Eguchi," an amalgam of other band members' facial features and another's voice, had her own online bio, interests, home prefecture, and—most unsettling—a *massive* fan base. Massive enough that deep digging by these fans eventually exposed the digital trickery and resulted in a minor backlash, though tempered by the sheer impressiveness of the videography.

More impressively and more abstractly, another Japanese company—Crypton Future Media—in 2013 held a massive live concert where for three hours the audience screamed for national pop idol Hatsune Miku. Miku is a perpetually 16 year-old schoolgirl virtual persona combined with a Yamaha Vocaloid synthesizer application. Not only is her visage artificial, her very pitch and cadence are computer-generated. There is no vocal artist behind Miku; she is entirely unique, while simultaneously being readily available to anyone for $149 USD (¥9800). She has a set height and weight, age, birthday,[10] even a recommended vocal register and favored keys. She appears on Television and web advertisements, stars in several cartoons and video game series, she even has her own add-on program so fans and professionals can combine her vocal synth software with visual animation dance software, creating organic and original routines from preprogramed "knowledge" of fluid movement and gravitational physics, just as a trained performer would learn new routines. Program her to perform something impossible and she'll fall. Tell her to sing a pop song in her somber timbre and it will sound horrible. She is *limited* in the same capacities as a human. She is artificial, yet she is Real; fake, yet true. She lives in that perpetual immortality of perfect celebrity, something usually attainable only by those who die young before burning out.[11] Arguably, Miku is more Real and more human than many living celebrities.

The idea of the Manufactured Celebrity is not particularly recent, though it's certainly become more nefarious of late. Public figures have always been keenly watched by media, and the boom of 24-hour television and internet news certainly leaves plenty of airtime to cheaply fill, but the earliest I can personally recall an admittance of viewer culpability in the *process* of celebrity would be the 1997 death of Princess Diana. It seemed the first time anyone had had to admit that the rabid manner in which we were constantly waiting and watching for certain famous persons directly affected their lives. Fame had always strained musicians and movie stars; catering to the masses had always been a strategy, sometimes even an unhappy circumstance, but Diana's death felt like the first time *everyone* had to collectively admit we were partly culpable in creating and eradicating our own public icons.

The notion itself at first glance is straight out of Marx: if the artwork (the performance art of being a celebrity 'character') can be

Girlpants and Gasoline

mass produced, then its originator (the living person) becomes alienated and abstracted from the finished product (the image). "Who you are on the inside" ceases to matter insofar as every living person you are likely to run into already has a preconceived notion of who you supposedly are. This is why certain celebrities spectacularly flare out in psychological breaks pertaining to identity issues, before attempting some sad "rebranding" "comeback." This is why we marvel at the few former celebrities who quietly bow out of the public eye and maintain reasonably average lives into adulthood, until the inevitable "Where are They Now?" digs them up.

This is also why Destiny Hope was a nice little girl, why Hannah was an artifice, and why Miley no longer has any idea who the fuck she is.

---

[1] It's worth noting Cyrus's ultimate moment of defloration: the day Disney replaced all her performance credits on iTunes with "Hannah Montana."

[2] In Cyrus' defense, it should be noted that salvia divinorum is commonly used in religious ceremonies and has a reputation for short, safe, non-recurring effects including euphoria, lucid dreams, sleepiness and a deep, spiritual awakening. It is also entirely legal in California and Cyrus was of age for its consumption at the time her video was recorded. Still, I'm pretty sure her dad wished the "I'll Beat Your Ass If You Screw Up Like That Lohan Girl" clause in his daughter's contract hadn't expired after she turned 18.

[3] Or iTunes. That seems much more likely.

[4] Potentially, it's less unreasonable to hate Miley Cyrus for anything she's produced under her own name since parting ways with Disney, taking the reigns, so to speak, and commercializing her own image with clothing lines and solo albums. Really, I can't imagine *anyone* that successful *not* wanting to cash in at least a little on their own ideas. That might actually have been more commendable than becoming the face of someone else's cash cow.

In a Halloween interview for the now-defunct MileyWorld.com in 2009, when asked which Jay-Z song was referenced in her clothing line's theme song and hit Summer single "Party in the U.S.A.," Cyrus openly responded, "I don't know. I didn't write the song, so I have no idea. Honestly, I picked that song because I needed something to go with my clothing line," later adding, "I have never heard a Jay-Z song," and, "I don't listen to pop music." Admitting her 'art' was a business and openly bashing her own genre was the strategic equivalent of knocking over a set piece on live television after shooting herself in the foot cleaning Chekhov's gun. Luckily for Cyrus, no one apparently reads MileyWorld.com.

[5] Just six slots below Mouseketeer-turned-singer Christina Aguilera, and twenty-four and twenty-six ranks below Disney alumnae Hillary Duff and Lindsay Lohan, respectively. Still, she was thirty-four places behind Amanda Bynes and and thirty-seven behind Michelle Trachtenberg, proving once again it's better to have worked at Nickelodeon. That Britney Spears and Taylor Swift both made the top 25 is just further evidence anything below the Top 10 is really little more a hodgepodge of cleavage.

[6] Fellow Disney alumnae Selena Gomez, Ashley Tisdale, and Vanessa Hudgens trailed in the Top 10, at positions 2, 7, and 9, respectively. For reference, singers Rihanna, Katy Perry, Taylor Swift, and Beyonce were 3, 11, 13, and 14. *Kate Upton* was only 8.

[7] Korean news animatics, anyone?

[8] Can you actually recall *why* certain celebrities became initially famous? The novelty of "Seinfeld" was often quoted as being "a show about nothing." Since Paris Hilton and Nicole Richie, fame has been talked about as and end unto itself, rather than the product of some labor. Essentially, we have mass-produced celebrity to the point it has been abstracted beyond function or intrinsic value. Louis Althusser would have a field day with that one.

[9] The general consensus was a suspected variation on the Pepper's Ghost illusion, whereby an image is projected onto a half-mirrored surface thus appearing to occupy a certain location in a real volume.

[10] 5'2", 93 lb., August 31, 1996.

[11] Ostensibly, Miku has simultaneously 9 and and infinity of years before she can join the 27 Club.

GREEN DAY: EVERYTHING THAT IS WRONG WITH MODERN AMERICAN THEATER

(And How It Is Saving the American Stage)

I recently attended an evening showing of *Green Day's American Idiot* on Broadway. Why did I do this? Because it was my mother's birthday. My mom has listened to Green Day for longer than I have, for longer than most of the audience in that theater–the younger ones who really shouldn't have been viewing material of that maturity–have been alive. My mom owns a physical copy of "1,039/ Smoothed Out Slappy Hours," that's how cool she is. Once year when I had no idea what to get her for Mother's Day I gave her $20 in a CD case so she could buy the then-imminent release of the new Offspring album.

Incidentally, my mother has also gone through four copies of *American Idiot*[1]. So yes, she bought herself tickets to a real Broadway show for her birthday and the show she wanted to see the most was *American Idiot*. She invited me along because, frankly, she didn't know anyone else who could appreciate juxtaposition of high theater and internationally acclaimed pop-punk. Being a gentleman, of course I accompanied her.

These following facts are what make American Idiot better

than any play in recent memory, though conversely they are also what will destroy everything we have come to expect from good theatre:

1. **There is plenty of cursing** - Both in the songs and in the (sparse) original dialogue, there is nothing classy or farcical about it. Like in much of punk's early history, vulgarity is primarily for shock value, though this in itself is a conveyance of raw, unrefined emotion, something usually only achieved in musical theater through emoting or big words. In this respect, *American Idiot* is closer to *Titus Andronicus* than *Hairspray*.

2. **Most of the audience already knows the words** - You never have to listen too closely if you already know what the lyrics are telling you. Except for Disney musical with puppets and other adaptations, only theater nerds know the lyrics and story to modern plays before seeing them for the first time. Most Victorian plays, meanwhile, were either topical or retellings of the classics, stories well known to the public.

3. **You can walk in wearing jeans and a t-shirt** - Hell, they have sharpies lining the entrance so you can sign the walls of the St. James Theater as you enter. Something is very wrong about this, but I have to admit it feels good as a young, hip person to own a piece of a historic building like that. The lack of necessitating perceived class amongst the audience makes *Idiot* phenomenally more accessible to the public, who as noted is already familiar with the source material, if only through having heard "Wake Me Up When September Ends" eight thousand times on the radio.

4. **YOU CAN DRINK IN THE FUCKING THEATER** - I can't stress this enough. There are *multiple* bars inside the building on at least two different floors and, yes, alright,

Girlpants and Gasoline

they're insanely overpriced ($17 for a cocktail and a beer), but frankly the bartenders are looking for tips and get understandably loose with how much liquor they sling. Here's the kicker, though: they let you take your drinks *into the show*. You can drink *during* a Broadway performance. I was ecstatic to find a bar inside, then livid that I couldn't drink at what was, essentially, a punk rock show, then finally dumbfounded and reverent at learning I was mistaken. Not only is drinking accessible to the audience more commonly than not, it is intrinsic to the youth culture of the show as it once was to those who attended performances as "groundlings" at The Globe theater. Shakespeare knew the promise of alcohol. It makes good plays seem even better and it makes bad plays seem tolerable.

This is where I reiterate my point to drive it home. *American Idiot* contains within it both the death and revival of Broadway as an entertainment form. It is fun, it is youthful and more importantly it is *accessible*. It grabs a whole generation of audience members at once, rather than subsisting on those few theater nerds until a new generation ages and becomes conservative enough to start attending the theater because it reflects well on them.

It's the very point of the show that that same aging process is somewhat inevitable, that those characters who do not die or fade away are forced to compromise who they once were and enter into positive relationships with the rest of society in order to ensure their own survival. If legitimate theater is to survive longer than print media, it is going to have to adapt its form into something other than a loose collection of rehashed pop cultural references. While that's all *Idiot* really is, it's *Idiot*'s abandonment of past conventions that sets it apart from old theater and among a new breed of performance.

That and it doesn't hurt that *Idiot* has enough sex, drugs and rock & roll to pull in a heteronormative male audience for the first

David E. Zucker

time since *Evil Dead: The Musical*[2].

---

[1] The first was a burned copy I bequeathed her when I bought myself a real disc to support the band. The second was one she bought for the same reason, which ended up partially melting in the car's CD player because she refused to listen to anything else for three months. The third, which replaced the melted copy, became so played out after two years that it had to be frisbeed into the garbage for interminable, constant skipping.

[2] Really. That was the manliest modern play I could think of. Every other joke revolved around *The Wedding Singer*, *RENT*, or awkward analogies to "Shakespeare In Love."

O' CANADA

The summer after I graduated high school my cousin got married. This became a tremendous pain in the ass, as my friends Jay and Mike and I had been planning a celebratory trip to Canada, leaving from New York on what worked out to be the day *after* my cousin's wedding. In Maryland.

After much finagling, my mother and I made great time, driving from New York down to Maryland in just three-and-a-half hours. Then we realized we'd left the formalwear sitting in a garment bag back home, so we turned around and made great time back to New York from just outside Baltimore. After that we spent seven hellacious hours making the trip down all over again, arriving at the hotel just before midnight.

The next day there was a wedding, good food, uncles embarrassingly dancing to Shania Twain's "I Feel Like A Woman," and grandma nearly set the reception hall on fire trying to dowse a small candle fire with her cocktail. All-in-all it was an entirely uneventful and uncharacteristically pleasant family gathering. As such, we

David E. Zucker

immediately bailed on staying another night so that I could enjoy waking up at four the next morning and sitting in the backseat of a Ford Taurus for another seven hours on the way to Montreal.[1]

Now, there is a very good reason why any and all of this seemed like a worthwhile venture at the time. You see, Montreal is part of French Canada. Since Quebec keeps failing to secede from the obvious tyranny that is Canada, it likes to assert its independence by, among other subtle jabs, undermining Canadian national standards and mandating a legal drinking age of just eighteen, a full year lower than the other Canadian provinces. This was very important to us, as at the time Jay, the baby of our trio, was approximately eighteen-years-and-four-days old when we gassed up the Taurus and set out for shenanigans.

Aside from lunch at an A&W restaurant–a rarity for lower New Yorkers–the trip Up North was relatively boring. With a bladder-bursting wait at the border, Canada appeared to be nothing more than an enormous tease, beckoning us with her free health care and her easy access to genteel (but vaguely European) cuisine, libations and linguistically accented harlotry.

Sitting in traffic with nothing to sate either our curiosity or our kidneys, blasting "O' Canada" and "Enter Sandman" from the car stereo, we mused over the little epigraphs on Ontario license palates. We made out *"Je me…"* before realizing that none of us spoke French. Also, no one had bothered to pack a French dictionary. Why would we? We were Americans. We take three years of high school Spanish and consider it worth the effort if a year later we remember enough to get our orders correctly placed at a McDonald's Drive Thru. Shockingly, for the duration of our stay in Canada we would be forced to act like young, stupid American tourists, which is exactly what young, stupid American tourists don't want to look like.

With resignation we accepted our predicament and, with tails between our legs, inched our vehicle in the general direction of a native of this strange and wondrous land. We pulled up to a Range

Girlpants and Gasoline

Rover.

"Hey! *Hey!*" we shouted, desperate for the Canadian's attention. *"What's your license plate say?"*

"What?" The man was understandably confused. This is not a question most people ever find themselves asked in their lifetimes. 'Pass the ketchup?' absolutely. 'What does your license plate say?' not so much.

"Your license plate!" we pleaded. We could just make out the words, now. *"'Je me rappellerai!' What does that **mean**?"*

The Canuck starred blankly into space, apparently trying to remember what, if anything, was scrawled across his car's plates. Conceding that there *must* have been *something* written there, he embarrassedly shouted back "... I forget!"

"What?" we asked over the din of traffic.

"I forget!" He shouted. It was here the Ontarian's wife tapped him on the shoulder. Repeatedly. She whispered something in his ear and the man's face flushed, further embarrassed. He yelled to us, "I'll remember!"

"What?" we cried in unison.

"'I'll remember!' It means, *'I WILL REMEMBER!'"*

There was a brief moment as we three inept teenagers stared at an adult, a supposedly mature and successful man, a *father,* for God's sake, staring back at us and all of us together realizing that even the inspiration that is the Canadian public school system can produce a pupil who can reflexively name all twenty-two prime ministers in order but who cannot, when called out, recall his own language. But in his defense, he did have to learn *two of them*.

We sat there for a moment, two cars, two nations united in shared awkwardness, and then we laughed so hard both cars had to roll up their windows and drive away from each other.

There's something about Canada that makes it feel just like a giant United States-themed amusement park. Take Disneyland and mix in frayed remembrances of what New York City was like before Giuliani cleared out all the nudie-bars. Montreal's main street is *Rue Sainte-Catherine,* lined end-to-end with Disney Dollar currency exchanges, off track betting and touch-friendly strip clubs. In fact the only thing keeping Montreal from being completely terrifying is an air of friendship and welcoming. The bouncers and ruthless grifters all are warm and understanding, putting on their best smile for the tourists and making sure you never see the guy inside the Goofy suit. Mickey, meanwhile, is a charming homeless man begging spare change to buy his sick daughter and her incredibly ill dog their various meds because he's out of work and living on the street with Huey, Dewey and Louie.[2]

The problem with theme parks is that they're the cultural equivalent of light beer or a diet soda; yeah, it's *sort of* what you asked for, but you can taste the difference. Assuming Los Angeles is Pepsi and New York is Coke, Montreal falls somewhere in the area of Diet Cherry-Vanilla Dr. Pepper. Or Mr. Pibb.

A "petrol" station just inside Quebec offered gas priced at just $1.32, which we thought unreasonably low considering exchange rate and proximity to the border. Why weren't the Canadians gouging us? Could they really be so kindhearted?

Confused but praising our good fortune, we pulled up to the ludicrously tiny Canadian gas pump and–after deciphering Canadian octane ratings–began filling our vehicle with sweet, delicious fuel. We then watched as the cost began skyrocketing. What was going on? Had the exchange rate suddenly shifted? Had there been a terror attack on Ft. Knox? Were we back on the gold standard? God forbid, could the Canadian Dollar actually be worth *more* than an American Dollar?[3]

No, that was simply not in the realm of possibility. What we eventually deduced was that the price we had seen was in *Canadian* dollars per *liter*, which roughly equates to "pay-out-your-ass" Ameri-

Girlpants and Gasoline

can.

Wandering inside, trying to divine our bill by splitting it by eleven and multiplying by six, we encountered Canada's answer to Sling Blade, a gas station attendant who despite a laminated quick-conversion table for this express purpose taped to the front desk was not mentally equipped to give Canadian change for American cash. After the first awkward minute we deciphered the table out ourselves, then spent the next two explaining it to the attendant and left him about a four dollar tip for the privilege of getting the hell out of there. Mind you, that's four dollars *American*.

It was a pretty straight shot from the border to our hotel. We spent a good forty minutes in terror, though, before figuring out that US I-81/Route 35/7B/whatever *becomes* "Autorut 18" as one passes between countries. To save time, I assume, no one ever mentions this on any map or road sign.

However, once our brains achieved that state of permanent wariness and readiness to convert Canadian *to normal*, we began to have some fun. We deciphered a few new and interesting street signs[4] and then realized we could tell everyone back home that we "hit a buck-fifty" going down a straightaway on Canadian highways. Sure, that was a hundred-and-fifty *kilometers* per hour, but as dopamine began flooding our so recently panicked brain we thought kilometers were hilarious.

Despite a complete lack of English on any street signs and an equivalent lack of French on our directions, we did a fairly good job of making it through Montreal to our cheap hotel. Hotel Sainte Denis is a small establishment, right on the corner of *Rue Ste.-Catherine* and *Rue Ste.-Denis,* so that once you find your way onto Main Street it really isn't too difficult a task to get back from anywhere in the city.

The three of us had originally booked a room for four-to-five people, but with last-minute cancelations we found ourselves sleeping in relative luxury. The room featured two twin beds *and* a pull-out sofa. Without extra people crashing on the floor with all their clothes and overnight bags, the room seemed outlandishly large for the three of us. A full private bath opened next to the beds, replete with scratchy towels and tiny bath soaps. Atop the television set rested ticket books for four guests' worth of comped breakfasts.[5]

Oh, but the television. The T.V. itself was absolutely nothing remarkable. It was a twenty-seven inch generic brand unit, bought in bulk and stocked in every room of every hotel this side of the universe. However in Canada, television is *amazing*. The first thing we did after scoping out the room was find something we could leave on and stare at for a few minutes to try and recuperate from a seven hour car ride. Not sure of what there was to be had, we settled tentatively on MTV's French-Canadian equivalent. We spent about twenty minutes trying to guess what was going on in a French animated show about sixteen year old French kids tormenting a French Christopher Walken who appeared to be a French security guard at their local (French) mall.[6]

As we rotated turns taking showers, the program changed and we found ourselves watching "The Ashley Simpson Show" with French subtitles. We didn't even realize that Ashley Simpson *had* a show then, and we found ourselves still trying to guess what the show could be about, however this time it was more a philosophical quandary than an linguistic one.

Finally all clean and ready to get scuffed up in the Great Big City of Montreal, we were given the gift of seeing *"Pimp Mon Char! avec Xibit,"* which is exactly as ridiculous as its American counterpart.

As we unpacked our warmest summer clothes–Canada was rather cold in May–we monitored the FremTV video countdown. Number five was an utterly bizarre video called "Tri-Cul" by Les Cowboys Figrantes, a video about a taxi driver whose pregnant fare goes into labor and has to be rushed to the hospital, but every person along the way, including the newborn, looks like one of the three

Girlpants and Gasoline

band members not playing the taxi driver. Number four was Longue Distance's "Moudit Qu't'es Belle," which completely rocked.[7] Placing at number three was the number one video for all of the past week, some wacky video I've never been able to identify and can only compare to the girl from Evanescence singing a Taylor Swift piece in French while wearing a tutu, filmed in sepia-colored basements populated exclusively by abused children. How do I know they were abused? Because they wore casts and walked with crutches and hid under beds with teddy bears crying, while one held up a crayon portrait of a monster beating him labeled "Daddy." I should reiterate that this had been the number one video for *an entire week*. Thankfully, this video had been bumped from the top slot twice over, first by Green Day's "Wake Me Up When September Ends" (which was played out from radio air before it even had a video) and then again by "The Speed of Sound" because the new Coldplay album came out that day. This was the point at which I decided I could not completely respect a nation that adored Coldplay that much that readily. After so much French pop television I had a sneaking suspicion that I was experiencing the same kind of overly-immersed confusion a poor Paraguayan child might feel at finally getting a scholarship to study at UCLA and realizing everything he sees on American TV seems decadent and in poor taste. I scolded myself for judging an entire nation on just its cable programming and vowed to give Canada another chance. It is statistically unlikely I would have done the same if we had instead come across French-Canadian VH1.

Children born in New York's Greater Metropolitan Area learn the Five Rules of Visiting A Major City:

1. Do not look up. It will make you dizzy and mark you as "touristy", a prime candidate for mugging.
2. Do not take pictures of the tall buildings. You will further look like a tourist, deserving of getting mugged.

3. Always look like you know where you're going, like you've lived a block away your entire life. Helpless looking people get mugged.
4. You are the only person on Earth. Treat all other pedestrians and most vehicles as invisible and jay walk whenever possible. This furthers your outward senses of both belonging and resilience, decreasing the likelihood of getting mugged.
5. Keep ID, a debit card and cab fare in cash in a separate pocket from your wallet/purse, just in case you still get mugged.[8]

In what daylight remained, our first day in Canada, we indulged in behaving as regular tourists, getting our money changed into crisp, flamboyantly colored denominations, wandering about with our necks craned in awe and just generally getting our bearings so that when darkness loomed we would be able to uphold the Five Rules and ideally not get mugged.

We spent a few hours visiting the Montreal Museum of Modern Art because we A) legitimately wanted to see some fancy art and, B) recognized it as a plausible alternative to any of the other places we'd visit when our parents asked us what we did all weekend. Securing a few souvenirs in advance, we meandered our way back to the hotel, exploring the city as much as we could while still waiting for all the bars to open.

Stepping out onto the sidewalk in front of the Hotel Sainte Denis is kind of like stepping over the Mason-Dixon Line, or at least what a Yankee Bastard might assume stepping over the Mason-Dixon Line would be like were we ever in the unfortunate circumstance of finding himself in such a place. Turning right, one can walk downhill into the docks and straight into the frigid waters of the bay. To the left, however, one has the option of turning again onto *Rue de Sainte Catharine* and entering any of the many bars, porno-shops, and strip joints that line the roadways. The better option—in daylight at least—is

Girlpants and Gasoline

continuing straight up Sainte Denis Street, opposite the docks. After a
few generic municipal businesses and a taupe cement parking garage,
the paved road and alleyways transition into immaculately maintained cobblestone. The buildings begin to look like Old London,
one-story homes stacked three-high with no continuity of architecture
or appearance. Minutely tiny staircases on the sidewalks wind up,
across brownstone faces to whitewashed front doors flush against
second-story facades, a mile of civic engineering designed either by a
madman or a genius, either of whom likely played a lot of Tetris
during lunch breaks. Most of these cramped apartments have long
since been converted into small, private boutiques, hookah bars or
expensive bistros, the kinds of places that spell 'shop' with an extra
P-E. Because they're *fancy*.

Walking up *Ste. Denis* I offhandedly mentioned that it should
be our goal, a gentlemen's bet, for one of us to cast aside the air of a
tourist and be mistaken for a Native Canadianite. As an extra chal-
lenge, it should be a true Canadian who makes the error. It was in one
of the small, ground floor boutiques precisely eighteen minutes later
where a young, attractive Canadian woman saw me replace a hat
stand that Jay had knocked into and asked if I could tell her how
much some scarf cost, assuming I worked there. If there is one thing
I do well it is blend into the urban hipster scene. Also, I apparently
ruin bets.

Interspersed with these bohemian locales are some rather ritzy
"adult novelty" shoppes[9] and approximately eight-hundred and
thirty-seven *bajillion*[10] head shops. We entered one the latter at
random and stared in wonderment at the copious variety of gravity
bongs and hydroponic apparati, multi-lingual instruction manuals,
secret-compartment-possessing soda cans and bongs made from
WWE collectible Steve Austin sippy cups. The owner, a lanky, long
haired American-expatriate-turned-legal-Canadian, came over to talk
to us. With courtesy and politeness worthy of a native Northerner,
and unlike every other drug dealer and smoke shop proprietor I've

David E. Zucker

ever met, that we obviously did not intend to buy anything from him did not phase this man in the slightest. He did not try to steer the conversation towards the selling points of *this* seven-foot rotating hookah over *that* one. Truth be told, after we mistook a macramé frisbee for a French beret, the owner spent a good forty minutes discussing the widening quality-of-service gap between Canadian and U.S. healthcare systems. This of course led to a conversation on the ineptitude of various world leaders named Bush, in which we felt awkwardly apologetic and were quick to point out that we viewed said C-student as an inaccurate portrayal of how the majority of educated persons viewed foreign and domestic policy, and moreover an inaccurate portrayal of an educated person in general.

This is not what we came to Canada to talk about, however. We did not drive nine hours for a forty minute discussion of socialized medicine. Upper *Ste. Denis* is merely something akin to California; it is fun to visit and the food is delicious, but it's a little too pretentious even for New Yorkers.

Let us be clear about the reason we decided to vacation in Canada of all places. It is the reason all underage American kids visit Canada: beer. Our parents, both tacitly and explicitly knew this. It was, after all, the same reason *they* drove to Canada in 1978. There was nothing they could do about it. They had no moral high ground; they could not forcibly impose hypocritical will on legal adults with valid drivers licenses, and frankly I believe they knew if we did not practice getting drunk then, we would be ill-prepared to get it right when we arrived at college orientation next Fall.

The trick was, we had somehow illustrated to our parents that while we may have frequently engaged in dumb, reckless behavior, we were through sheer experience at this point well versed in crisis management, penal law and basic first aid. As contrary as it sounds, though we may have been the *cause* of more trouble than others our age, parents seemed to universally recognize that there was no one

Girlpants and Gasoline

our age more qualified to *handle* any trouble safely and responsibly.[11]

In the trunk of our car, we had had the forethought to pack a spare duffle bag and an empty plastic cooler. With these items we could purchase beer and ice at whatever passed for a 7-Eleven in Canada, then get responsibly hammered in the safety of our hotel room. It was a brilliant plan, save for the surprising difficulty in finding a store that would sell beer to barely-legal kids with foreign drivers licenses at 6 p.m. on a Sunday. After getting horribly turned around on the autorút we found a small, grimy corner store and managed to hand a middle-aged Pakistani couple about $35 American for Solo cups, four six-packs of Molson's and something red called "Fruity Tornado Twist Malt Beverage," which we instinctively dubbed "Bitch Beer." We returned to our hotel room and, after locating an ice machine, ended up sitting around the room playing drinking games until we decided to move out around nine.

Wandering the streets, we passed large men in suits tempting our libidos with "*GirlsGirlsGirls*" like extras from a high-budget, big-studio parody movie mocking low-budget, independent exploitation films. I fully expected Shaft or at least Samuel L. Jackson to spring out the back of a Cadillac and high-kick three pimps and a hooker.

Passing what might have been the sketchiest looking alley I have ever encountered, we entered into an establishment. I hesitate even to call this place a "bar," as the only bars I could see were located on the outside of the stucco-faced building's one window, the interior view obstructed by a black curtain and a single neon sign proclaiming "BAR." It was a dive several blocks closer to the pier than any other, but small and out of the way enough for us to test our newfound superpower of legally obtaining intoxicants.[12]

Jay ordered a round of Heineken at the bar while Mike and I tried to establish our manliness by setting up a game of Cutthroat on the ragged pool table that sat comfortably within running distance of the front door. We drank, we told off-color jokes, we played with heavy balls and pointy sticks. Our first foray into public drunkenness was a smashing success. Jay returned from ordering our second set of drinks positively jittery, fearful and disgusted, demanding we finish our beers quickly so we could leave. I assumed he had made the mistake of existing in front of the booze shack's more colorful clientele.

Rather, while waiting on our drinks Jay was propositioned by a remarkably unattractive whore better suited to working sailors on shore leave than sober teenagers, and about this I must be clear: she was not merely an uncultured woman who I abhorrently call a "whore." This was a strung-out, toothless leather handbag who, while attempting to grope him, asked Jay if he was "Looking for a good time."

Jay *was* looking for a good time, which is why we hastily beat it out the door and were half a block away before he explained why it was he had needed to call a retreat. Still, we had engaged Lady Booze and survived, having shown remarkable tact and fortitude in running away from ugly, crazed hookers. She would respect us for that. All we needed now was to find a more up-scale establishment in which to get thoroughly hammered. Preferably one without whores.

For our upstanding courage we miraculously chanced upon the least Canadian oasis we could conceive of: O'Hara's. We had found an Irish pub in French Canada. It was like unto a dream, a dream of sticky wooden bars and shockingly immaculate bathrooms. My compatriots meandered towards the former as I stumbled downstairs to the latter, where I gleefully listened to talking vacation adverts hanging just eye-level above the facilities.

By the time I returned I was already a full drink behind. Not desiring to be outdone so easily, I ordered a couple rounds of Irish Car Bombs[13] from a pretty, Mid-Western American bartender. As I was downing the last curdled dregs from Jay's second car bomb, the increasingly attractive bartender turned to me and asked, "Oh, I never

Girlpants and Gasoline

checked your ID, did I?" Having been indisposed while Mike and Jay were carded, I had somehow escaped notice.

"Oh. No," I said. "I'm used to it, though. I was always the older one who looked young, but once I grew a goatee people just assumed I'm so much older." This was my first experience with unnecessary drunken rambling. I was beginning to divulge facial hair trade secrets, to a very nice looking woman no less, who quite clearly wanted to settle down and calm the tortured rebel within my soul. But I could be tamed by no woman, and so I wrapped it up and tried to appear less than absolutely shitfaced. I don't think I succeeded, but she never did ask for my ID.

From O'Hara's we went across the street–after tipping our lovely hostess well of course–to a more trendy club, one with bouncers. Also, there were nachos. I had drunkenly gotten maybe, slightly, just a little lost on the trip across the street and gone inside to find Mike and Jay. As I did not see them, I left to use my cell phone away from the din of rattling club beats, whereby my friends were very nice and came outside to get me. Walking in with them a *second* time I was finally carded. It was glorious.

At this point, however, my memory starts to get a little purple colored and I can't recall much other than all of us stumbling back to the hotel, all the while repeating "Mounties can't arrest you for public drunkenness if you're trying to walk home or to your hotel.[14]"

By the next evening we had a pretty good grasp of how to comport ourselves while drinking in public. After a modest pre-gaming session Mike, Jay and I walked far too far down the highway and got lost. Splurging, we secured a cab and asked to be taken directly to wherever the clubs were. Far from *Rue Ste.-Catherine*, we found ourselves on some type of boardwalk. Cafes and watering holes strung up with decorative lights lined either side of the rolling cobblestone pavilion. Tremendous crowds gathered in loose herds waiting for admittance into the Old World architecture. We chose the longest line with the most attractive girls.

Fairly sloshed already, standing in line for an hour became something of an ordeal. A part of me was angry that I had left the only book I brought into the country back in our hotel room. Another part of me, the one that willingly goes out to clubs, was angry it couldn't beat up the first part of me. All the parts were angry we hadn't brought more beer.

A step ahead as always, Jay left us guarding our position in line to peruse the few shops that remained open along the stretch of cantinas. He returned maybe fifteen minutes later with a very shady looking 40-ounce beer in a brown paper bag, which he unironically guzzled in line until it was confiscated. Understanding but still miffed about losing his beer, Jay started commenting on how weak and skinny the bouncers looked at this club. He remarked, "I could take him," with sureness as he pointed to a particularly tiny, stoic bouncer, who immediately proceeded to high-kicked a rowdy and lecherous bar patron in the face. He kicked him *in the face,* staying perfectly still, save for raising one foot off the ground and putting the sole of his boot up a man's *nose.* The angry young man flew from his perch atop the club's stoop, out the doorway and sprawled on the ground unconscious. The skinny bouncer straightened his t-shirt, turned, went inside and decided for us that we would play nice with the other children once we got inside.

Inside, it turns out, was not all that impressive. A single, open room about the size as a small storefront, there was a dance floor to one side and a raised area with chest-height tables but no chairs. Beer was available by pitcher, but nothing else. What we were experiencing wasn't actually *inside.* For our exorbitant door fee, we had received color-coded wristbands and entered some kind of tiny pre-club where we were to drink pleasantly while waiting for the color of our wristbands to be called. This invitation, then, would grant us entry into the club proper. It says much for your bar when there is a forty-five minute line to get into the place where you wait to get into

Girlpants and Gasoline

the actual establishment.

But dear Lord, it was almost worth it. Climbing a flight of stairs into the main building, the walls opened up and left us staring at a bar easily ninety feet across worked by a half dozen tenders. It simply lined one wall of a full warehouse and continued out of sight behind a writhing sea of pretentious white kids. What was once a coat-check to our left had been converted into a dollar shot booth. Beer flowed double-fisted by the pitcher and the dance floor, with its mass of sweat and flashing colors, looked like the Vanilla Ice scene from the second *Teenage Mutant Ninja Turtles* movie. Lights shown down from the ceiling two stories above, suspended by industrial scaffolding.

Not being big dancers, Jay left to buy beer while Mike and I ascended to the second floor, a third-story balcony ringing the lower level and overlooking the catwalks and smaller lighting equipment.

As far as I remember, we didn't talk much. Or at least *I* didn't talk that much. Though the music was overwhelmingly loud, I can just recall Jay and Mike having something like a conversation between our efforts to get hammered on Molson's Dry. After the first two pitchers Jay couldn't walk and, having a girlfriend back home, sent Mike down to the dance floor with myself as designated wingman.

Considering how extraordinarily drunk and nearsighted I was, I retained enough of my former intellect to realize this was a very bad idea. I lost track of Mike almost instantly, then turning around a few times, I had to almost immediately give up my search as I discovered I could no longer point in even the general direction of gravity's pull. I remember walking[15] back up the stairs and through some small miracle finding Jay. Mike reappeared several minutes later.

Apparently, Mike had rather politely asked a reasonably attractive girl to continue dancing as she was, however to also acknowledge him in some manner while doing so. Her response was, shortly, unreasonably bitchy. Pretty people are allowed to be bitchier than ugly people[16], however, because apparently others *enjoy* looking at pretty people. As true men, we took offense and commiserated with our fallen brother. I was appropriately reprimanded for failing in my responsibilities as wingman and letting him get shot down alone, but it was generally agreed that it had been a suicide mission from the get go.

As if to reaffirm the adage "Bros before hos," our circle of drunkenness was invaded by a true master of the sport, a drunken college dropout who wandered into our conversation, badmouthed the prissy skank two floors beneath us and drank directly from his own pitcher. As Don McLean's "American Pie" blasted out of the speakers directly behind us, our mystery companion began singing and hugging us and throwing our hands into a circle like a deranged and inspirational hockey coach. He continued this for the song's full eight-and-a-half minutes. Hands stinging and Weird Guy still on the periphery of our vision, we carefully and quietly made our way out the bar and pointed ourselves vaguely towards Hotel St. Denis.

Now, up until this point I have withheld a certain piece of information regarding Montreal and that is this: Elaborate Story Homeless Man notwithstanding, solidly eighty-five percent of Canadian street beggars are punks. I do not mean to say that they are bad *people*; they probably are, but that is beside the point. What I mean to say is that approximately fifteen percent of Canadian bums are homeless beggars, who–according to the one who followed us for several blocks inquiring as to the financial situations of beggars in New York City–are all bi-lingual and earn upwards of $200 per day squeegeeing car windows. These people are fine. Any one of them could be shipped down to the states and, barring simple things like work visas and state board licensing examinations, secure work as high school French teachers. They *would*, however, be forced to take a pay cut.

Girlpants and Gasoline

The remaining majority of Montreal's transient population is *literally* anarchistic, black-clad, chain swinging, combat boot wearing punk rockers. They have stepped out of 1989 onto *Rue Ste-Catherine*. Pale, unshaven teens and twenty-somethings line the streets with their large, spiked boots and their pasty, overweight girlfriends with unnaturally colored hair.

These are young people who reject the current socio-political systems and throw away their wallets and their expensive possessions to live a hard and therefore meaningful existence. Basically, it's a perfect imagining of Hell for Yuppies and aging Baby Boomers.

We, however, were eighteen and wearing Iron Maiden t-shirts, semi-immune, possible heirs to their street corners. Young beggars were kind enough to remember our faces and not ask us for cash more than once. One looked us right in the eyes at two in the afternoon and asked, "Hey, can I get two bucks for a beer?" He was honest. So honest, in fact, that we readily forked over about four dollars.[17]

It was refreshing not to hear rehearsed sob stories. This boy earnestly wanted a beer and had zero money. He saw that we could understand that desire, that–like him–we did not resent panhandling, just bullshit. Punks may seem fairly insane, but they are to a T a fraternity of the brutally honest. They were willing to interact with us, talk to us. We met a congenial couple who lived on the street with their dog and had no idea how or when they would find their next meal. They met each other following a metal band on tour. Rather than part ways and go back to their parents' houses, they kept with the tour until they ran out of money. Montreal was just the city where that happened. They were Gypsies now.

These people remain on the streets after dark, obviously, as they *live* there. We, on the other hand, after nightfall became drunken, foreign buffoons who squandered *tens* of American dollars on door fees and *imported* American beer. Understandably, this was the point in the evening at which we lost our magical ability to walk

David E. Zucker

amongst hardened, angry nomads unfettered. Appointing the least drunk of us the responsibility of deciding whether or not there were cars on the roads in front of us, we stumbled arm-in-arm[18] for several blocks towards our hotel.

At first I began to notice a group of teenaged punks huddled outside an abandoned multiplex cinema with several ragged dogs mulling about around them. One of their group appeared to be attempting to underhand a three-foot, partially decorated Christmas tree and catch it on the foreclosed cinema's darkened marquee. As this was late *May*, the tree itself was the color of cardboard and hemorrhaging needles. The young man did not seem to be *angry* at the sign or the movie house, or even the tree; he just seemed concerned with gradually relocating the tree up top of the sign. Also, he seemed keen on *glaring at us intently.*

Jay, usually the most roguish and outwardly violent of our group, was currently stumbling between my stumbling to his left and Mike's stumbling on his right, and–despite his black Metallica t-shirt–was generally looking neither roguish nor violentish. Across from the theater, maybe a half block down, passed another small group of punk-bums. They walked between us and, in passing, one threw up his leg back and sideways, lightly kicking Jay in the leg and missing his scrotal region by about a couple inches. With a steel-toed boot. Now, in hindsight the intent is fairly obvious. At the moment this happened, though, being drunk but responsible we just assumed it was our fault. Jay apologized, citing that he did not wish to start anything and that he was just delightfully plastered.

It took a few seconds for Jay to rescinded his apology, as it came to his attention that he had just been purposefully kicked by "a lousy bum." Mike and I spent the next several minutes trying to keep Jay calm and moving (if not actually pointed) in the direction of our nice soft hotel beds. We kept him as calm as we could, explaining that we were currently being eyeballed by no fewer than three distinct groups of punker-bums, a good fifteen-to-twenty people ready

Girlpants and Gasoline

to defend without hesitation their local brethren. We placated Jay as best we could, the copious amount of Molson's Dry in his stomach working against us. What finally kept him from turning back was something Mike said.

"Jay," he said. "He's a fucking *bum*. He's *homeless*. You're going back to a nice warm bed. He. Has. No. Fucking. *Home*."

Understanding seemed to glimmer in Jay's eyes. Perhaps he was slighted, yes, but he had a better station in life. In fact, he was happier and had a better work ethic than this grimy asshole. Sure, he could be an asshole too, but at least he'd be *a* clean asshole. And, having actually *seen* the film *SLC Punk!*, Jay knew that most of these transients were ideological poseurs who would eventually get bored, go home, get a job, get a haircut and get a real life. Jay calmed, laughed and proceeded to walk maybe a quarter block before slamming his fist into the stucco wall erected in front of a renovated storefront. Two minutes later Jay asked us why his hand hurt.

Back at the hotel when we wrapped Jay's hand in a washcloth from the bathroom we dipped into melted ice water from our cooler. As we shut the lights off to go to sleep, Jay asked for by now the fifth time why his hand was bleeding, to which Mike and I concisely told him, "Jay, you got *kicked* by *a bum*."

In the morning we approached our homeland like real men, with painful hangovers and a minuscule quantity of a controlled substance wedged into an empty Sprite can in the dashboard cup holder.

"Where you heading?" asked the most depressed customs agent-slash-border guard, seemingly fully aware of the uselessness in guarding America against Canadians.

"Uh, we're going home," we answered. "We were on vacation."

"Vacation?" The guard raised one eyebrow. His left one, I believe.

David E. Zucker

"Yeah, we just graduated so-"

"Do you have anything to declare?"

"I … I don't think so?" We looked around, wondering if souvenir keychains were declarable items. "Like what?"

The guard sighed. By rote, he answered, "Food. Perishable items, souvenirs?"

"Oh. Uh, I think we got some sandwiches left in the cooler? And some souvenirs? Like a shot glass and a teddy bear."

"Teddy bear?"

"For my *girlfriend*." Jay was a little insulted. He may not have been America's answer to Bill Shatner, but, damn it, he could at least treat a girl well.

The guard then said the following; it wasn't a question but it also wasn't a warning or a simple statement. It was, in effect, a proclamation of plausible deniability by someone completely disenchanted by the way his career had played out. What he said was this:

"And you kids have no illegal drugs on you." We replied in the affirmative, sealing our conspiracy of shame and laziness. Had we replied that, yes, there were *some* drugs in the car, just a little bit, then that would have eaten up whole chunks of both our day and the guard's, and really none of us wanted that, so it was really for the benefit of *everyone* in the grand scheme of things.

The guard let out the longest, most defeated and disheartened sigh I have every heard a man utter. We watched his burgeoning beer gut let itself out as the he looked down solemnly at his switchboard and with all the enthusiasm of an aging carnie working the last functioning ride at Canada Land, pressed the button that would raise a wooden barricade and usher us home. As we left, he muttered to us and to no one in particular, "Well I guess *my* job here is done…."

By comparison, two days earlier we had been grilled for a good ten minutes by a petite Canadian woman who demanded to know our exact reasons for staying a weekend in her country and proceeded to check our birth certificates against computer records.

Girlpants and Gasoline

Apparently, "It's legal for us to drink there," isn't an acceptable answer and, "For the museums," just comes off as incredulous.

Sometimes I worry about my country. And by 'sometimes,' I mean "usually."

---

[1] Thanks, Mom.

[2] Actually, that last bit really happened. There was a beggar whose sob story included a sick child and her sick dog, a deadbeat wife, a lack of housing or employment and mentioned needing both food and unnamed medicines for both the child and canine. I've talked it over with Jay and though we can't recall exactly how it made sense in context, we both agree that a group of space aliens had been worked tangentially into the story. It was very elaborate. We gave this homeless guy money *twice* during our stay, out of sheer respect for his creativity and commitment to the material. Unfortunately, Canadian quarters are the same size as Canadian $2 pieces, so as I forked over $1.65 American Alien Guy was elated, almost as surprised by my generosity as I was. But, hey, it's not like I could have asked for *change*.

[3] Since the Canadian Dollar has out-valued its American counterpart for some time now, I'm legitimately shocked Canada doesn't give us more shit about it. I mean they're *nice* people, but we frankly deserve it. All that's really changed is that *now* when I get a Canadian penny in my change at a McDonald's I get *excited* for earning that extra $0.006.

[4] "No Bikes" and "No U-Turns" and "No Commercial Trucks" made sense, but I still maintain there was one that meant "No Station Wagons." Apparently Canada hates station wagons.

[5] Real breakfasts, not a small buffet but true, sit-down meals including the usual egg and toast dishes (from what we could translate), but also the fanciest, most bizarre take on cinnamon toast I have ever come across. It was essentially a large, home-made cinnamon roll, cold and hard, sliced through in the center and arranged like a sandwich around what I think was some kind of warmed-over, homemade heavy cream cheese, topped with rocks of pure Columbian cinnamon. Everything came with fresh juices and water from the most beautiful blue, expensive-looking glass bottles, the empties of which not coincidentally became the tables' centerpieces.

[6] This show, I learned after years of fruitless searching and then serendipitously seeing when it aired in the U.S., was *6Teen,* which *is* about sixteen year old Canadians and *does* take place exclusively in a mall that *is* guarded by a thinly-veiled caricature of Christopher Walken. It was picked up in part by Nickelodeon and later by Cartoon Network and was hilarious, partly because international copyright laws gave the show leave to mention and openly mock American media juggernauts.

[7] This was singularly the most interesting French-Canadian pop-punk I'd ever heard, which doesn't say much but it was also great by American standards. It was angry and

David E. Zucker

happy and self-aware and laughing at its own pretense and when I finally got the lyrics translated months later it turned out to be French Emo. The line, "Curse you for being beautiful, you rock'n'roll girl" is not hardcore in any language.

[8] This rule is also useful for drinkers who know they cannot be trusted to save enough cash to get home from the bar.

[9] Some might have passed for simple boutiques upon cursory examination. They were classy. One, though, had a sign that was just a giant anthropomorphic condom, so that one not so much.

[10] I am approximating.

[11] Case in point: when we told our parents we were out playing ultimate frisbee until 1 a.m., were were legitimately on a field with a flying circle. We were not drinking or smoking or soliciting loose women. However, when a man named "Crash" tells you to go to the E.R. for stitches, you grab the disc, pack some gauze and get in the car.

[12] I am reasonably certain an *infant* could have obtained liquor in this place. With out-of-state ID.

[13] Like other "bomb" drinks, drop in this case a shot glass of half Jameson's whiskey and half Bailey's Irish Cream into a half-filled pint glass of Guinness Extra Stout. Chugged immediately it will taste like ice-cold Yoo-Hoo.

[14] More recently, New York has similarly abandoned charges of public drunkenness, in an effort to create a viable alternative to drunk driving. 'Drunk *and disorderly*' however is still an offense, so just don't be an *asshole*.

[15] More like a controlled fall, really. And what is walking if not gracefully falling and catching oneself repeatedly in the same direction? Regardless, what I did was not in any way graceful, though I recall only once slipping on the stairs. Points for style.

[16] The equation is $B = (P{\bullet}IQ)$ where acceptable bitchiness is inversely proportionate to how pretty a woman is multiplied by how intelligent she is. This is why we get angry when celebrities fail to use up their bitch points and turn out to be genuinely nice people. It's also why fat, dumb assholes are so annoying.

[17] Even the drug dealers were nice, though they work on an entirely different system of code words than American drug dealers. Metric, I suppose.
Us: "Yo, you have any tree?"
Drug Dealer: "What?"
Us: "Bud? Grass? Weed? Green? Dope? Sticky? ... *Pot?*"
Drug Dealer: "Oh, sorry, man. Dry. YOU WANT SOME COCAINE THOUGH?"
This happened at least three different times. Apparently Canadians do a lot of blow.

[18] For balance, not camaraderie.

BEER CHASER

When my grandfather fought in WWII he once signed a piece of paper for the Air Force, taking possession of a $238,000 Boeing B-17 "Flying Fortress." He thought it was ridiculous that in 1945 he wasn't allowed to vote, but they let him sign for an entire plane while feeding him stimulants and depressants in tandem. But the upside, he would point out, was that back then you were still allowed to *drink* at 18.

Honestly, I have real mixed feelings about setting a drinking age. I've read studies insisting that cultures where drinking wine is common from a young age have lower instances of alcohol abuse, drinking-related diseases and drunk-driving, while usually maintaining longer, healthier life spans. I've also read that these cultures normally don't count the frequency of their McDonald's visits per week.

Legitimately, I've been 18. I wouldn't trust many 18 year olds to drink responsibly, but I also know that irresponsible underage drinking is at least in part a result of not being able to legally drink. A glass of wine at dinner isn't underage drinking in Italy, it's dinner.

David E. Zucker

Stolen Budweiser and watered-down rum drunk in a cemetery on Halloween out of a flask you swore you only bought for orange Tang, well, that's always going to be underage drinking.

But I almost see that as a good thing. Your late teenage years are when you get in all the practice you need to make sure you know how to drink by the time you're actually old enough to do it. Bars filled with wasted teenagers serve a societal purpose: they keep the annoying teenagers out of real bars. By the time I was of age I knew my favorite drink, my favorite shot, my favorite beer and my favorite ways not to throw up in the morning. Society couldn't *function* if college graduates were just learning how to hold their liquor.

Underage drinking teaches you duplicity and *confidence* at the door, calligraphy and forgery with your identification ... *chemistry*, for God's sake. Chug before it curdles. Never mix acid with dairy. "Liquor before beer, you're in the clear. Beer then liquor, you'll get much sicker." I once brewed my own ale in a plastic bin under my bed using a dorm stove and a wire hanger. Hell, I got free tech support with a direct line by helping a guy reverse engineer proper syphoning technique. Also, it got me a bottle of mead.

ON FILIAL PIETY:

MAX GOOF, STEVO, AND RECONCILING INDIVIDUALISM WITH PARENTAL VALUES

"So the other day, I was naked with a finger wedged deep in my ear and snacking on rice cakes soaked in soy sauce while balancing on one foot on a pyramid of delicate china cups and saucers, and I thought to myself, 'Oh my God, I've become my father!'" - Bob Roth

'Do we inevitably become our parents?' It's a question that plagues my dreams at night, somewhat less frequently than the zombie apocalypse but drastically more terrifying. I'm at least prepared for the zombie apocalypse. I own large knives, I can theoretically use a firearm, I am learning to ride a motorcycle (towards and away from explosions), and frankly I'm prepared to die a meaningless death because I don't have the stamina or cajones to survive the fall of civilization. I'm barely prepared to survive the fall of my wireless coverage.

David E. Zucker

What I'm certainly not prepared for is giving up my humanities degree and becoming a project manager for a huge, multinational telecommunications company. That's what my parents ended up doing. Three bachelors and two masters degrees between the two of them. And what was my father's choice career advice? "Be a stock broker. Work your butt off for fifteen years and retire by forty." Sage wisdom from a Philosophy/Psych major.

Yet is it natural, after asserting our independence and striking out on our own, to return to the traditions and behaviors on which we were raised? In exploring this notion we have to examine values of both parent and child, and I can think of no more entertaining and accessible way to do this than through the lenses of two films vastly separated in genre and audience, but closely related by the theme at hand: 1999's SLC Punk! and Walt Disney Pictures' 1995 "Goof Troop" spinoff, A Goofy Movie.

Within A Goofy Movie there are two father-son relationships: predominantly Goofy and Max, but also that of their next door neighbors, Goofy's time-honored foil Pete and his son P.J. (Pete Jr.). While Goofy is a caring and loving father, Pete is the martinet, keeping his son in line through fear and discipline, prescribing an endless series of chores throughout their vacation, which exclusively serve either Pete Sr.'s personal extravagances or to reinforce his supremacy. In giving Goofy parenting advice, he refers to this as "Keep[ing] them under your thumb." P.J. stands at attention before his father, comes when called to perform tasks, but otherwise avoids spending time with his father, in private company going so far as to openly resent it. Pete's strict mode of parenting does not create the same kind or strength of bond that Goofy and Max develop throughout the picture. Contrarily, Pete doesn't even give his son a personal name, instead bequeathing P.J. his own name in an attempt to forcibly mold his offspring into that same identity.

Quite similarly, in SLC Punk! we are introduced to protago-

Girlpants and Gasoline

nist Stevo's father, who–representing a traditional upbringing–encourages Stevo to go to law school and finish his education, particularly the very college and law school he himself intended. His seemingly lax attitude and post-graduation recommendation of "and then do whatever" is counteracted by the on-its-face ridiculous notion to first "try it for four years and if you don't like it, quit." Stevo's parents duet an advisory call-and-response: "Be free," "Be practical," "Go to Harvard," "But have fun," "Be an individual," but he should get a haircut. Politely and honestly, Stevo begins to criticize his parents for abandoning the "Cultural Mecca" of their former home in New York City and with it the ideals of the 1960s, exchanging them for a white picket fence lifestyle in Salt Lake City, Utah. He later calls his father a hypocrite for being Jewish yet driving a German Porsche, for applying to Harvard Law School under Stevo's name and, more seriously, for divorcing Stevo's mother, saying "Y'know, you gave up a good thing in my mother, Sir." Though he admits to "just busting his balls," Stevo's disagreements with his father's values are sincere.

The major problem with the question "Do we become our parents?" is it inherently holds a bias towards the child's perspective. That is, it assumes becoming like one's parents is of necessity a bad thing: losing aspects of one's personal identity, becoming subservient and filling assigned roles is a loss of both freedom and self for an individual and (partially) a psychological death. It is an imposition few children appreciate as they grow into adulthood.

But rather than accept this value judgement, we should first examine the values of our parents. If, like 98 percent of children in the United States, a child is not abused, his parents can't have been too morally reprehensible. Likewise, if a child lives in the suburbs like roughly half the U.S. population as judged by the 2006 census, she probably does not have much to rebel against other than being as drearily average as P.J. or Stevo's families.

David E. Zucker

While these are certainly certain parents not to use as role models, that is not to say becoming like one's parents is universally a poor life. Max Goof shares equally with P.J. and Stevo an apprehension of becoming like his father, or at least fearful of acquiring the genetic and personal traits he has grown to view as embarrassing, unhip or otherwise unenlightened. The film opens, in fact, with a nightmare sequence in which Max's idyllic pastoral plane morphs into a grove of thorns as he frightens away his love interest, Roxanne, by undergoing a werewolf-like transformation into his own buck-toothed and clumsy, HYUCK!-ing father.

Throughout the movie, though, Goofy's values are not so terrible. Much the opposite, he prides himself on leniency and understanding of his son's feelings, preferring over Pete's rules and harshness family togetherness and traditions like father-son vacations and the family's secret fly fishing "perfect cast." Excepting perhaps his father's taste in music, Max's greatest issue with Goofy is not his ideals or even his clumsiness, but rather that he feels smothered under his father's constant and frequently embarrassing presence in Max's personal life. This, Max feels, hinders his development and growth as an individual and so he comes to view Goofy's ideals, though wholesome, as an imposition of parental will as antagonizing as Pete's.

The issue at hand is really a value judgement placing a child's accrued morals and experience over those impressed upon him by his parents earlier in life. Learning that our parents might be in possession of values not openly hostile to our own, perhaps even well-conceived and tested by decades of experience beyond our own, the question takes a different shape: "Are our values, if different, really any better than those of our parents?" If our values are no better than those of our parents, even in line with theirs, what can be said of our growth as individuals?

Max Goof feels like a nobody in his high school, at worst a loser to be picked on, at best fading into the background. However he

Girlpants and Gasoline

also believes that he does have some innate coolness. If he can do something outlandish and cool he would win the heart of Roxanne.[1] The act he chooses is to interrupt a school assembly with a pyrotechnic-laden lip syncing performance while dressed as Powerline, his world's most popular pop star among children his age. Quite literally, Max abandons his own identity and adopted a preexisting, suave, well-liked persona which is at once rebellion against the role of his father's son and conformist in regards to his peers, which does manage to impress the latter at the expense of the former.

This is of course the impetus for the story's main conflict, wherein Goofy attempts to "save" his son's soul from a life of delinquency while Max tries to maintain his own independence and coolness. Yet Max maintains a relatively stable moral framework, managing to enjoy time alone with his father away from social constraints. When Max alters his father's road map to culminate not in a father-son fishing vacation, but at Powerline's rock concert in L.A., it is for him a devastatingly conflicted choice, but one he feels necessary to preserve his identity from being crushed under being his father's will. It is an open deception of his father, something Max is not at all comfortable with and its exposure opens an emotional rift between the two.[2]

SLC Punk! features a protagonist much more openly dislikable by mainstream society. A punk rocker and anarchist in 1985 Utah, Stevo's values are frequently directly opposed to the ordered society to which his parents belong, often seeking it's partial or total dismantlement. He rebuffs his parents' advice for living a normal collegiate life, calling them hypocrites for leaving a societal hub of counterculture, for exchanging their ideals for high-salary jobs and expensive cars, for rejecting through the dissolution of their marriage even the very notion that true love can conquer all. In one of the film's most quotable moments Stevo asserts his contrarian lifestyle: "I am the future of this great nation! ... I love you guys, don't get me wrong … but for the first time in my life I can say 'Fuck you!'"

When asked by his father why he even bothered to major in pre-law at community college, Stevo replies, "I studied law because I wanted to learn how completely full of shit your life's ambition really is." Yet Stevo's actions undercut his mission statement of no-rules rule. The very fact that he did attend college is evidence of this and, as his father points out, even if he achieved success by cheating for four straight years, Stevo cared enough about grades and his status in society to desire and receive high marks in all his classes. Becoming conscious of this duality, he thinks to himself:

> My dad was right about one thing. Why'd I do so well in school? I didn't want to. I mean, I tried. I tried not to give a shit. I knew it was all bullshit and they were trying to mold me into cannon fodder for their wars. And I knew that meaning lie elsewhere, but somehow I studied. Somehow I got the grades and now somehow **I** was accepted to a fucking Ivy League school–the last place on the planet for a guy like me. I mean I wouldn't even go there unless it was to set it on fire.

Stevo further muses that when he actively takes part in fighting the local rednecks he is partaking in a hierarchal system that is in essence a scaled-down version of war, creating the same Us versus Them mentality underpinning nationalism, colonialism and the irrational, self-propagating discourse surrounding Edward Said's "The Other." He recognizes that this is a system very similar to the one he rejects as being antithetical to his anarchist doctrine, admitting he can offer no explanation for this. While actively engaged in a fight he concedes, "Everything has a system, even me. I was following nature; nature is order and order is the system."

So what happens if a child's alternative value systems collapses? In Max's case the act of duplicity he was already feeling guilty about is discovered, resulting in an impassioned argument with his

Girlpants and Gasoline

father, wherein Max argues that his negative actions come about only in trying to distance himself from his father and grow as a person. Their argument grows so heated that they begin to ignore the physical world around them that the two, along with their car, tumble over a cliff and into a rolling river. Surrounded by water and cut off from any other 'human' influence, Max and Goofy are forced to deal with each other directly:

> Goofy: You even lied to me.
> Max: I had to! You were ruining my life!
> Goofy: I was only tryin' to take my boy fishin', okay!?
> Max: I'm not your little boy anymore, Dad! I've grown up now! I've got my own life!
> Goofy: I know that! I just want to be part of it!

It is at this Max realizes distancing himself from his father is causing as much turmoil in their relationship as Goofy's attempts to forcibly bridge the divide. Father and son then come to a mutual understanding via a stirring musical number we shall address shortly.

Stevo, however, is a bit older. Having graduated from college and now living outside his parents' homes, we get to see his alternative values play out in the larger world. Out with his casual girlfriend Sandy, Stevo runs into a fellow punk from high school named Sean, who has since accidentally overdosed on acid and, thinking his mother to literally be a Satanic monster, attempted to murder her with a kitchen knife. Following a brief incarceration in a psychiatric facility, Sean is now panhandling on the street, "FUCK YOU" scrawled across his torn clothes and incapable of the basic human interaction necessary to support himself. Sandy's immediate advice, to which Stevo readily agrees? "You should get a job[3]." When faced with real hardship, the punks' first instinct is not to thrash the system and take what they need to survive by force, but to accede to that system's structure.

Seeing what can happen to people close to him who follow his

David E. Zucker

same anarchistic doctrine to the extreme, Stevo muses:

> "I couldn't even look at the guy. I felt a pain in my stomach. I couldn't take it so I turned my back, just like everybody else … It really fucked me up. Not Sean, but turning my back. Ignoring the truth. So what'd I do? I dropped acid with Sandy in Highland Park as to further ignore the truth."

Stevo openly admits to running away from the harsher elements of his lifestyle, implying that he might be cognizant of his desire for some of the protections offered by an ordered society. As Stevo's personal relationships begin to crumble, he sarcastically mouths off to his best friend and roommate Bob for falling in love and considering marriage and a family and running a business. "You're a poseur," Stevo says. "Only poseurs fall in love with girls. You're a poseur." While he quickly reneges, the thought has been vocalized. Stevo cannot reconcile his own desires with his current lifestyle.

The final death of Stevo's ideology comes with the untimely loss of Bob, at which Stevo expresses denial, grief, guilt, anger and bargaining all in the space of about ninety seconds. He insists, "Only poseur's die," but this is a clear fallacy in his belief structure and an argument that cannot resurrect Bob. As realization dawns over Stevo, he laments that he has lost his last real friend, muttering simply, "Oh man. Oh jeeze. Oh my God. I wasn't ready for this. I wasn't ready." It may be quick, but in this short line of dialogue Stevo has completely discarded anarchism, invoking first Man, then in minced-oath Jesus Christ, then finally God.

Stevo's penance as the prodigal son of family and tradition is to shave his perpetually blue, spiky hair down to a Spartan buzz cut for Bob's funeral and don in place of his usual t-shirts and razor blades a mournful, black suit. "If the guy I was then met the guy I am now," Steve says, "He'd beat the shit out of me." In the final voiceover he openly repudiates his former values and agrees to return

62

Girlpants and Gasoline

to traditional society:[4]

> So there it was. I was gonna go to Harvard, be a lawyer and play
> the goddam system … I was my old man. He knew….We were
> certain that the world was gonna end, but when it didn't I had to do
> something, so fuck it. That was me: a troublemaker of the future …
> You can do a lot more damage in the system than from outside of it
> … I was nothing more than a goddam trendy-ass poseur.

Though Stevo is pushed through only the most begrudging
reconciliation with traditional family values, Max comes to terms
with his father in a much happier, prototypically Disney fashion.
Following their shouting match atop the barely-floating car drifting
down river, Max and Goofy sing a duet through which they learn to
respect and even admire each other's differences. Max chimes in
regarding his father, "Though he seems intoxicated/He's just highly
animated," to which Goofy reciprocates with, "Your moodiness is
now and then bewilderin'/And your values may be–so to speak–
askew." Max concedes that his father acts only out of love and he
will honor that, while Goofy agrees to respect his son's emotional
space and allow him to experience parts of life on his own. Newly
reconciled, Max and Goofy have an (assumedly) cherished heart-to-
heart between scenes in which Max catches his father up on his
teenage angst and the Powerline predicament. Goofy then decides
that the only appropriate way to end their ordeal is to get Max on-
stage at the Powerline concert in L.A. as promised, thereby negating
his son's lie to Roxanne and getting Max some sweet, sweet dog
lovin'[5].

However, before Max can gain any real reward from this new
acceptance and openness with his father, he must first be tested to see
if he is deserving of his father's boon. Max needs a trial-by-fire. Or
waterfall. A trial-by-waterfall. That works too. They're already
floating downstream through a canyon, after all. Goofy cements his
place as a good father by getting Max to (relative) safety fairly

David E. Zucker

quickly, but Max has to find a way to save his father from tumbling over the falls. With only a fishing pole and tea set floating nearby, Max saves his father by correctly executing the family's secret "perfect cast," despite how ridiculous it makes him look in the process. The adoption of family tradition over 'looking cool' firmly plants Max's morality back in traditional Disney soil. Alive and safe the loving father-and-son duo can now go break into a stadium, sneak on stage, ruin tens of thousands of dollars worth of electronic equipment and then utilize the perfect cast as an original dance step, bridging old and new generations in mutually destructive and illegal havoc broadcast over national television.

In denouement, Max reveals to the disturbingly nubile Roxanne[6] that he does not in fact know Powerline, whereby she informs him that she was instantly attracted to not his faux-suaveness or his looks, but to his hereditary HYUK, the very laughter Max had feared, loathed and attempted to hide from her. This happy Disney ending validates Max's choice of family tradition over contrariness for its own sake, whereas SLC Punk! takes the darker approach of effectively punishing Stevo's reluctance to accept his own parents' values. Though Disney understandably portrays this choice as thoughtful and worthy of praise, and though SLC Punk! rather callously defines parents' values as being akin to the 'lesser of two evils,' both convey the solid warning that values which are old and not well understood by some does not make them necessarily wrong in the long-term. More often than not these values endure because they are things we too will come to believe in time, when we better understand the world and are not immediately terrified of possibly, maybe, slightly, even remotely becoming even a smidge like our parents. But Zeus help me if I turn out anything like my father.

---

[1] A small sampling of appropriately aged heterosexual middle-class males seems to indicate that Roxanne is by far one of the most common cartoon characters to give little boys funny feelings for the first time. To my knowledge, however, none of these

Girlpants and Gasoline

participants have actually engaged in romantic relationships with real dogs.

^{Sub-footnote} Yes, everyone in the *Goof Troop* universe is a dog. Goofy's "raucous laugh" predates his screen debut, but he was in his first appearance credited as "Doofy Dawg." You see that "W" in "Dawg?" Yeah, Walt Disney was a real O.G., son. *Word*.

[2] A rift that can only be closed with a car-rafting musical duet.

[3] Officially the third most parental saying in the English language, right after, "When are you getting a haircut?" and "Ask your mother."

[4] So long as he can cause trouble by pissing off judges as a lawyer.

[5] Remember: they're dogs. Still. This hasn't changed in the last four footnotes.

[6] Seriously? What's up with that? I haven't been this confused since *Clueless*. (Paul Rudd is just too awesome. Every man bro-crushes on Paul Rudd.)

ON MY FATHER

The greatest advice my father ever gave me was after his third glass of Wild Turkey whiskey when he turned to me and said, "Son, *sexual attraction* ... in *any* relationship–even a brief one–is directly proportionate to *emotional commitment...*" then he began to take a swig from his tumbler but caught himself, adding, "*Except in this case.*"

At this point he proceeded to throw back his glass and wander off to order round four. When I tell this story at parties, this is the part where I paint a broader picture of where we were when he dispensed this wisdom by pretending I had had the nerve to respond, "Gee, Dad, this is the best bar-mitzvah ever!"

I remember this vividly. It was my little brother's bar-mitzvah and only a few minutes later I had to insist he stick to *either* encouraging me to hit on the Jersey skanks in attendance *or* continue referring to them as my "cousins." (Through multiple marriages he also insists that we are also related to the late Ayatollah Khomeini. I can only verify a passing relation to Ron Popeil, but no one ever wants to

Girlpants and Gasoline

talk to him because he's kind of an ass.)

My father, for his part, remembers none of this. However, he *does* readily take responsibility for it because it paints him in a humorous light and quote, "It sounds like something I'd say."

The other great advise my father gave me was "become a stock broker, work your ass off for twenty years and then retire at 40." You tend to have to pick and choose with him.

OF HITLER AND JOSH PECK'S ASS

I try to picture Groucho Marx hobbling around a kitchen set, bent over and with legs akimbo, trying to stick his cigar into the center of a tasty apple pie *à la* the *American Pie* franchise, and something just feels a bit off. Though greasepaint eyebrows and pie-fucking don't necessarily seem very far apart on the comedic spectrum of shits and giggles, there's a modicum of *class* missing from Jason Biggs' penile pastry shenanigans. While Marx's own *Duck Soup* and Charlie Chaplin's *The Great Dictator* are no less silly at times, they carry stronger moral and political messages than "teenagers worry about getting laid," which resonate throughout the pictures, in terms no less sophisticated than high drama or the orations of great leaders like Roosevelt or Churchill.

These films hold a measure of timely validity encasing the attitudes of their day. While I can't argue that the mainstreaming of awkward teenage sex *wasn't* a prevailing attitude of 1999, modern comedies *do* tend to communicate a less-than-sophisticated message,

Girlpants and Gasoline

exploring at best our already postmodern understanding of the world, and at worst nothing at all. A few special films manage to be a bit more thought-provoking, not just passively reiterating the same popular themes of its genre and era but actually adding to the conversation. To make the comparisons for this analysis as ridiculous as possible, I'll sample against the Marx films the 2008 comedy *The Wackness*, starring Sir Ben Kingsley and the indomitable Josh Peck, as well as Josh Peck's indomitable glutes.

Shot in 1933, the Marx Brothers' *Duck Soup* is currently ranked by the Internet Movie Database among the top 250 films of all-time. Take note: that is the top *films*, not *comedies*. While certainly silly, absurd, and at times even vaudevillian, *Duck Soup* is a comedy more in the sense that Shakespeare's *As You Like It* is a comedy; utilizing a troupe of regulars, the film features an ensemble cast of heroes and villains, clowns and kings who cavort in court and prance in pasture and generally engage in wild engagements, both on the battlefield and in the bedroom. Common sense plays second fiddle a serious commitment to lunacy, until all the characters–regardless of affiliation–are brought together in the midst of great conflict out in the middle of nature, and in one last twist of circumstance are miraculously saved. Fanfare then breaks loose and the women sing. Which story was I just describing? If you said "*Duck Soup*," you obviously haven't been paying attention to what you've been reading, which is a real shame considering you're only three pages in. If you said "As You Like It," or "Both," then you're a smug bastard thinking you can get on my good side by spouting my own ideas back at me without any real understanding of the point I'm making. Well good for you, at least you're playing the game.

Comedy in *Duck Soup*, as much as in any Victorian play, is both an end (in that it pleases the audience) and a means to express some other (I won't say a necessarily "higher," but certainly a valid) idea.

David E. Zucker

Filmed and released during the Great Depression, between "The War To End All Wars" and the next war obviously brewing, *Duck Soup* is a treatise on the absurdity of war and the ineptitude of Old World politics. As the story opens, the country of Freedonia is announced to be imminently bankrupted by foolish bureaucrats and their complicit party leaders. Worse still, the nation is under constant threat of war from its ambitious neighbor Sylvania. Mrs. Teasdale, wealthy widow of the country's late president, agrees to bail out the nation on the sole condition that the reigning president resign and Rufus T. Firefly, a beloved countryman, be instated in his place. This reasonably shaky[1] set-up is the same sort of *deus ex machina* one would see were someone of reasonable political and financial stature to bankroll a true grass-roots movement in the federal government.[2] Beloved by his people for God only knows what reason, Firefly (Groucho) immediately announces in song, chorally backed by the Freedonian senate,[3] that his first acts shall be to abolish all types of fun and happiness while hypocritically committing every act he plans to outlaw. To thunderous applause he promises, "If you think the country's bad now, just wait 'til I get through with it."

Further satirizing the ridiculous ways by which government functions, results overshadow method and ideology. Firefly rouses the nation into patriotic uproar and, instead of covertly ousting a shifty foreign dignitary, plunges into all-out war with his country, over what was initially name-calling between two gold-digging politicians both lusting after a widow's fortune.

Self-serving and criminally under-qualified political appointees run the war into the ground, switching allegiances for personal protection until Freedonia's leaders find themselves trapped in an old farmhouse well behind enemy lines. They defend their poorly barricaded position by *bonking* over the head with a 4x4 ceiling joist each enemy soldier as he breaches their perimeter. The third of these officers happens to be the same foreign dignitary who

70

Girlpants and Gasoline

helped engineer the war, who also readily surrenders *the entire war* to avoid being pelted with *fruit*.

Coming from a time of massive financial losses, the opening sequence in which Mrs. Teasdale essentially bends the Freedonian government to her own questionable devices was not too far-fetched a possibility. To save a country immediately, the best long-term strategies are not likely to win over much support. It is still the case that economists decry politicians' hindrance of public works programs and massive governmental spending, while politicians rally majority support for short-term fixes which only temporarily keep more money in the pockets of their constituents. Though a vast majority of President Franklin Roosevelt's public works organizations were disbanded or severely cut during the following Truman administration by a conservative supreme court that labeled them socialistic and unconstitutional, during the bleakness of Depression surrounding the production of *Duck Soup*, these programs were hastily approved as godsends. In times of desperation, personal and political principles often sway to need.

More substantially, it's the lunacy of war being decried in *Duck Soup*. Just fourteen years after the end of World War I, the America to which Marx and his brothers were catering was still a country believing it had just fought and won the "War to End All Wars." Yet already, the film's makers could see that it was not the Alliance system itself that had predicated the global conflagration of violence, but rather foolish, brutish, and often completely mistaken individuals who held power simply for the reason that they were financed for it. And just as the world was left more tattered and bitter following the end of the Great War, nothing of any measurable value is resolved by the conclusion of *Duck Soup*. The war is won, Freedonia is glorious and triumphant, and Rufus Firefly is a hero, having clearly won the heart of the rich widow Teasdale. However both nations are financially, militarily and bodily depleted by the war. Nothing is won, no borders change, and as the Fat Lady–Teasdale,

David E. Zucker

legitimately dumpy and the direct cause of the entire social upheaval–sings the Freedonian national anthem in a warbling operatic tone, everyone pelts her with fruit because they're tired of hearing the same old nationalist crap over and over again.

Though it was released just seven years after *Duck Soup*, Charlie Chaplin's *The Great Dictator* provides an even more startlingly accurate portrayal of the American zeitgeist during the inter-war period. As *Duck Soup* satirized the follies of government and war, Chaplin's film more directly confronts the question of why governments so often betray the will of their own people. Chaplin portrays with frighteningly accurate detail and a keen understanding Adolf Hitler's then-contemporary rise to power in Nazi Germany, and the political stirrings in Europe that would soon erupt into a second World War.

The plot itself follows two parallel stories, intertwining only ever so slightly prior to the film's ultimate scene. The first opens with Chaplin portraying an unnamed Jewish barber during World War I[4], a soldier of the Germanic nation of Tomania, who is put into a coma heroically rescuing an intelligence officer named Schultz. Though Schultz survives, the war is lost.

Twenty years later, The Barber has been cared for in a military hospital, suffering complete memory loss from his accident with Schultz through the last two decades. The chief comedic element is established in this: The Barber one day leaves the hospital and returns to the Jewish ghetto to reopen his barbershop, unaware that in his absence Tomainia has elected a fascist, anti-Semitic dictator in response to the political and economic turmoil impressed upon the country after the war's end.

The secondary plot revolves around the depiction of this Fuhrer, Adenoid Hynkel, a disturbingly accurate (though far sillier) representation of Adolph Hitler *also* played by Chaplin, and his political gaffs in trying to secure funding from a Jewish banker for an

Girlpants and Gasoline

expansionist war into neighboring Osterlich against the nation of Bacteria with which he signs a non-aggression pact.[5]

The insanity of an absolute dictator is succinctly put forth in a scene between Hynkel and his crafty minister Garbitsch, in which Garbitsch placates a worried and insecure fuhrer by describing the "perfect" world their machinations will create, where Hynkel rules absolutely. "A world of blond-haired, blue-eyed Aryans," they parrot back-and-forth. "Aryans ruled by a brunette." It calls to the blatant logical missteps of Hitler's own Nazi ideology.

Chaplin follows this with a cementation of the idea that a dictator is by nature a paranoid, power-mad lunatic, showing Hynkel playfully tossing an inflatable globe in the air, dancing with it as a gentle symphony plays. To Hynkel, the world is quite literally a toy. War, therefore, is merely the game by which he wins what he feels he is entitled to. The rights and lives of individuals–even his soldiers– are nothing but game pieces. He strips Tomania's Jewish population of their rights, then returns them to get his military funding. Once secured, he strips them again, also ensuring that he will never have to pay his debt to a banker who now has no rights. Simultaneously, he signs a treaty with Bacteria promising neither will invade Osterlich, a country lying between the two. Hynkel knows he cannot win a war against Bacteria at this juncture, but with his new funding plans to launch a blitzkrieg into Osterlich's capital, capturing the nation with a grand army capable of defending against and even conquering Bacteria in turn.

Meanwhile, The Barber and what friends he finds in the ghetto manage as best as they can to survive as Hynkel tightens control of Tomainia and oppresses its Jewish population. The Barber is saved from lynching by Schultz, who recognizes him and jogs The Barber's memory. For opposition to the invasion of Osterlich and his tolerant stance on Jews in the face of Hynkel's worsening ethnic cleansing policy, Schultz is branded a race traitor. He hatches a plot with other members of the Jewish ghetto to suicide bomb Hynkel's home, and

David E. Zucker

though they decide against violent opposition, their meeting is discovered. While most of The Barber's friends escape to Osterlich's countryside, he and Schultz are captured and thrown into a work camp.

As his friends listen to Tomania's worsening war of expansion via radio, The Barber and Schultz make a daring escape from their prison dressed as military officers. Cornered by the fuhrer's aides, The Barber is mistaken in likeness for Hynkel, while Hynkel, ostensibly on a hunting trip by the Osterlich border to allay suspicion of an invasion, is subdued by military police chasing The Barber and Schultz.

Entirely without effort, The Barber is ushered into the capital of Osterlich as a conquering ruler, where he is expected to speak before teaming masses and denounce free speech and equality, backed by a racist, ruthless military. Dumbfounded, Schultz explains, "[To say something] is the only hope we have." Chaplin, as The Barber, gives a rousing speech that demonizes the hatred and exclusionary tactics of fascist societies, expounding the idea that only through freedom and tolerance of difference and variety can the true wonders of human potential ever be expressed in society at large. He demands that no soldier ever raise his arms in hatred or anger, but only in defense of his common man. The movie ends as Chaplin calls out to Hannah, his estranged love interest, to look to the skies for the brightening days ahead.

Comedy is more form than function in these cases, a juxtaposition to the terrifying and tragic nature of war, a lightening of the mood to turn farce from what was in truth a great tragedy. Slapstick allows the protagonists and their merry bands to escape ruthless soldiers and intolerance. Tomainia's dictator is painted both as evil and as a buffoon, personally a weakling and a bit stupid, but also a master orator with unscrupulous (though highly efficient) aides at his side. Even with such a heavy satiric bent, it's disconcerting to see

Girlpants and Gasoline

such an exacting representation of Adolf Hitler committed to film *before* the U.S. had officially gone to war with Nazi Germany.

In giving his full speech, Chaplin completely abandons suspension of disbelief and with it any unfounded preconception left in our minds restricting comedy from being a work of substance. He goes so far as to remove from the audience even the task of deconstructing and understanding his work's meaning. Looking straight into the camera for the bulk of his oration, it is not The Barber detailing exactly what about fascism is gross and inhumane, what perils lie behind the curtain of ordered and homogenous peace won by expunging dissenting opinions, it is Chaplin speaking. It is a cry for responsibility and intervention in the fight for a just cause, happening at the very moment he spoke those words. It is the American Ideology in 500 words or less.

Having more or less accepted infinite diversity in society as commonplace,[6] what zeitgeist is expressed through current film comedy? Following the 1980s America matured out of its selfish teenager phase as a nation, and is currently personified best as what I would call an over-educated, postmodernist twenty-something layabout who can't focus at either his high-status internship or his low-level data-entry position because he's overly-involved in a messy break-up that left in question the fate of his band's amps, most of his t-shirts and the guardianship of a golden retriever named "Buster" currently still in his girlfriend's Eighth Avenue loft apartment.

America is no longer concerned with what it believes in. It decided firmly that it's perfectly fine for people to believe whatever they want, and thus it took all the fun out of believing in anything in particular. If everyone can be right however he wants, then no one will have the strength of conviction in her beliefs she used to have.[7] Movies, then, no longer focus on the lofty ideals and thought-provoking speeches of glory and ideology. More than asking "What do I believe in?" today's movies are primarily concerned with the ques-

David E. Zucker

tion "Who the Hell am I to believe in anything, anyway?"

The results are two sides of the same coin, assuming that coin features on both obverse and reverse a portrait of former teen actor Josh Peck.

On the one hand, we ask this question of ourselves and get a movie like *The Wackness*, starring Peck as Luke Shapiro, an eighteen year-old pot dealer in the city of New York circa Summer, 1994, who finds nothing in himself or the world to believe in. Luke befriends his client and sometimes-psychologist Dr. Squires (Sir Ben Kingsley), sleeps with Squires' step-daughter (Olivia Thirlby, the best friend from *Juno*), falls in love with her, shows us his ass, saves Ben Kingsley and grows up a lot. What a summer.

There is no slapstick in *The Wackness*. The closest things to "low" comedy are probably scenes in which Dr. Squires is trying desperately to feel like the young, idealistic rebel he used to be. Ostensibly he's trying to show Luke what a boy his age should be doing in life, but Luke sees only an old psychologist, graying at the temples and on every prescription he has access to because he can't deal with the fact that he and his gorgeous wife (Famke Janssen) haven't been in love in over a decade.

Humor in *The Wackness* is much more subtle, situational. Often it's awkward to the point where laughing is just a preferable reaction to crying and throwing up in the corner. Squires scrawling his signature across every thing in his house he would want to keep in a divorce, or partying for three days on amphetamines, barbiturates and every other pill he could get a hold of while his dog runs through the room with a note reading "Take care of me, my owner killed himself," hanging from its collar. True, there are lighter moments such as Luke practicing increasingly ghetto pick up lines, even the idea that he sells weed out of a rickshaw-style ice cream cart. Over family dinner Luke tells his parents and grandparents that he has finally decided to go to college for psychology, "Because everyone around me is so fucking crazy, y'know?" Given that we force our-

Girlpants and Gasoline

selves to accept every alternative ideology as a valid opinion, regardless of what we ourselves might find to be correct or objectionable (be that justifiable or not), how can an individual not go a little bit crazy trying to reconcile all the conflicts of thought around them?

Every comedic element in *The Wackness* is designed in such a way as to seem authentically "real." Not "The Real World" real, not even "Jersey Shore" real. *Legitimately* real. Like actual life, just as awkward, but with better dialogue. "He doesn't appreciate you." "How could you know that?" "He couldn't possibly." It *reads* the horribly awkward way everything you said to a girl sounded in high school. And that's incredibly awkward to watch someone else do. Repeatedly.

Frankly, I had no idea *The Wackness* was a comedy until I went searching for it on DVD. I didn't know what to call it because all it felt like to me was "true." My local media store had it filed under COMEDY. All one copy of it. The Internet Movie Database, meanwhile calls it drama. But just like *Duck Soup* and *The Great Dictator* it features scenes of rampant wit, a tinge of blue-humor and an otherwise absurd premise–that a young white boy from queens who's just a little too old to be watching *Ninja Turtles* would spend his Summer searching for meaning in his life, only to find it by *failing* to find it in friendship, love, or prescription medications. Similarly too, *The Wackness* ends with our protagonist speaking directly into the camera espousing exactly for us the meaning of his life. According to Luke Shapiro, if everything around you is–metaphorically–making you crazy, the best thing to do is to take up the study and treatment of those things that are already crazy. Study intently that which already surrounds.[8]

The other side of the coin is, unfortunately, something Josh Peck was also privy to. Earlier, I referred to Peck as a "former teen actor." I did this because his most notable role was as Josh, "the fat weird one" in Nickelodeon's "Drake and Josh," a Caucasian remake of the network's own "Kenan and Kel." Two friends are as close as brothers, despite one being a conniving ladies man and the other an incredibly awkward dork. In fact for the remake, they actually *became* brothers by marriage. It was the same as "One Tree Hill" and "The Brady Bunch" and a dozen sitcoms before it, a simple rehashing of tired, played-out comedy staples in a new packaging, occasionally updated to include references to more current celebrities and technology, packaged in thirty-minute bundles. The only goals are to make the most money for as cheaply as possible, while placating viewers who have become too depressed and overwhelmed by the plethora of conflicting messages already floating through their airwaves. Also, it gave Miranda Cosgrove a jumping off point.[9]

Drake and Josh is *Kenan and Kel* is Abbot and Costello is Punch and Judy and so-on. *Kenan and Kel* spun-off of Nickelodeon's *All That* while *Drake and Josh* spun-off from the same show's short-lived revival. It never even made an attempt at originality. That was never the point. Luckily, this time around the fat kid thought it best to avoid the secondary illnesses associated with obesity and lost the weight. Now he gets to show his chiseled butt without guffaws in real roles alongside Ben Kingsley, instead of actively ruining every new episode of *Saturday Night Live*[10].

Though the public at large tends to draw a divide between comedy and what should be considered meaningful, Oscar-worthy cinema, there has never been a comedy that wasn't also saying something serious.[11] Yes, it's much easier to deconstruct *Duck Soup* and *The Great Dictator* as uncanny representations of the American Way during their times, having had the benefit of seventy years on which to look back and create a proper context. And, yes, I'm sure that fifty years from now *someone* will look back on *something* as still being a stupid and worthless piece of celluloid trash.[12] But someone will also find something from these years to be marked as utter genius, a cinematic explosion epitomizing our generation's

Girlpants and Gasoline

entire existence as human beings. I'm just hoping it's an explosion of wit from someone like Tina Fey and nothing by Michael Bay[13].

---

[1] Likely just the most successful way of pitching "Groucho Marx is elected President of Europe" to Paramount executives.

[2] For example if Michael Bloomberg were to get tired of managing New York City and decided he simply wanted to buy up controlling stock in the rest of the country.

[3] Whose voices are just lovely.

[4] We can call it WWI in discussion now that we've established Europe had already started World War II. Time travel is neat!

[5] Precisely as Hitler signed a non-aggression pact with the Soviet Union so as to not have to fight a two-front war. At least not until he was militarily prepared to betray them.

[6] Or "accepting the postcolonial absorption of only the most amiable aspects of various cultures into modern Western-European society." Take your pick, really.

[7] Except for those pesky extremists and conservatives who never agreed that it *was* okay to be different in the first place, but no one can make them stop shouting because everyone *else* believes they have *the right* to shout. And people wonder why Americans prefer to get their news from comedians.

[8] God willing ~~and~~ you'll make a career out of this and make enough money to behave however the hell you want.

[9] Cosgrove's "iCarly" actually went on to be a huge success while the little sister from "Kenan and Kel" had a brief, simultaneous stint on Nick Jr.'s "Gullah Gullah Island" costarring with a six-foot, yellow pollywog.

[10] "The skinny one" in both cases made some pretty poor career decisions. Kel Mitchell's next largest roll was in *Mystery Men*, as a superhero who could only become invisible when no one was watching. Drake Bell appeared as some sort of Spider-Man knock-off in *Superhero Movie*, a box office bomb directed by the guy who wrote *Scary Movie 3*, which was directed by another guy with the incredibly sexy name David Zucker. I still didn't see it.

[11] Hell, even the "Movie Movies" are designed to mock (read: "cash in on") their respective genre popularity.

[12] Have I mentioned the Movie Movies?

[13] If Tina Fey got divorced and married Michael Bay, they would be celebridubbed "Fey-Bay." "30 Rock" would suddenly gain a massive special effects budget and Bay's movies would start being, well, *good*.

Transformers as an Allegory for Transsexuality in America

I had been reading an old, defunct webcomic called *Venus Envy*. It's an interesting premise, the daily life and somewhat unique trials of a 14 year old transsexual, somewhere a little less understanding and accepting than a liberal college campus. I highly recommend it, if not for the art–which is adorably ... er, *rough* for most of the series–but for the subject matter. The stories are interesting and have a perspective most cisgendered[1] people don't get to hear from barring a very special episode of "Glee." Eventually some of the more surreal elements take over and, as with any loosely autobio project, an actual plot emerges as a way of wrapping up the fictional bits, which kind of takes away from the slice-of-slice aspect. It's not bad, it's just a change.

Beside the MTF bisexual protagonist, there are a lesbian, about thirty other lesbians, a straight FTM transsexual, and a fairly straight transvestite, the last explained with a pretty adorable diagram of boys and girls who like girls and boys, or boys and girls, and the

Girlpants and Gasoline

occasional boy who likes girls but also to dress like a girl sometimes. The first lesbian remains generally confused. Essentially, if gender is performative and sexuality is an expression of innate desire, a straight crossdresser might be considered 'transperformative.'

But not transportative. That would be a body dysmorphic Transformer. Oh, yeah. One night while reading this I also fell asleep after watching a bunch of "Transformers" episodes. The two must have joined forces in my subconscious, because I awoke to a realization:

Transformers can be construed as a dissertation on transsexuality in modern America.

Now, before we continue, I should note that as a giant nerd I *know* on what Transformers is a dissertation. It's selling toys. Made by a Japanese company. Originally, a bunch of leftover toys they had lying around from a previous franchise. But hear me out. If there's anything I learned in Intro to Criticism, it's that creators get very little say in how we read their works, mainly because we read whatever the hell we *want* to see in past works, generally to help prove our own point. So what the hell, let's exercise some cognitive irreverence.

The over-simplified reading is Autobots and Decepticons, as well as all their various cousins and iterations since the 1980s, disguise who they are with a different but familiar covering. To say this makes them transgendered would be akin to saying an army sniper is a transspeciesist for wanting to dress up like a bush. *Camouflage* is not the same as *identity*.[2]

Transformation was developed–depending on continuity–as a covert military tactic, however it *is* a partially biological function. Transformers–silicon-based life forms–contain within them a biomechanical organ called a T-cog, which enables the process of transformation. Personally, I subscribe to the theory that this is a function of a high-energy reaction fueled by the fundamental element of Cybertronian life (a 'Spark') reconfiguring swarms of nanobots which are themselves the individual 'cells' of a Cybertronian's body … but that's a bit of a digression. The take-away is that transformation is an inherent property of a Cybertronian. It is not performative any more than respiration or, perhaps more aptly, *running* is to humans. However, the manner in which a Transformer *acquires* its alternate mode is a somewhat murkier matter.

Like gender and sexuality, a Transformer gains the quality of its "disguise" both biologically and socially. Cybertronians, when not crafted directly from raw materials by the ethereal tools of their godlike forebears (themselves creations of the multiversal singularity and embodiment of creation held over from the universe which preceded ours), are "birthed" as *protoforms* from biomechanical pods. These pods convey upon the protoform both locally acquired vehicle/animal mode and party allegiance.

Let me repeat that. While the *process* of transformation is biologically inherent to all Transformers, *what* they transform into and even the world views set down over their base personalities are impressed upon them by Ideological and Repressive State Apparatuses. They are literally *programmed* what to look like and who to hate.

It *is* possible for a Transformer to switch its alternate mode and even its affiliation, though the latter is quite rare. More often personal agendas have more to do with breaking allegiances than ideological or moral differences. Vehicle guises however are often switched as a result of a change in semi-permanent location, in order to better stay hidden. This process, however, usually requires "reformatting," which outside of Michael Bay's film universe, is a rather lengthy and resource-draining process requiring specialized machinery. (Or the multiversal singularity and embodiment of destruction, split from the original essence of the last being from a previous universe. Either/or, really.)

Girlpants and Gasoline

Yet Cybertronians seem to take reformatting in stride, as if there were nothing they could do about it. That's just the way outside forces make them. As much as Decepticons might prod at perceived lacks in a vehicle mode's performance, Autobots and Maximals know that it's a bot's character that determines worth.

Of course, according to Michael Bay all Transformers choose their own disguises, and they all choose either Chevy or GM makes because if you choose to change into anything *foreign*, you must be a spineless, capitulating, sissy-nancy *who hates America*.

Then again, that kind of over-performance just reeks of drag queens.

---

[1] Those whose self-identification of gender matches their biological sex.

[2] And *that* brings up a whole analogy to "passing" and staying closeted out of fear of societal repercussions.

MICHAEL BAY IS THE NATURAL EVOLUTION OF CINEMATOGRAPHY

Every so often I ask my grandmother what she thinks of the experience when she and her 90 year old friend buy one movie ticket each, and then sneak into two others afterward.[1] Color was a big deal for her. Sound was newfangled and hokey to her mother. So what does my grandmother think when she watches a car eject a young man, turn into a giant robot in front of her, shoot another giant robot that used to be some kind of Dodge she doesn't recognize, then turn back into a car and catch the tiny screaming fellow?

I really try to ask politely, hoping that one day she'll give me an answer like, "Well, I know it can't be real, but movies were *never* real. It *looks* real, which I guess is the new thing, but it's like seeing a movie, I guess. You just know that whatever is impossible is a cute trick designed to sell a story."

"How do they *do* that?" is all she ever actually says. Before I

Girlpants and Gasoline

can guide the conversation back the way I want it to go, mom usually interjects with, "Computers."

I think this is where we're all going, though. We come to expect the impossible in front of us every time we sit down to watch a blockbuster these days. Do you know what the big innovation for "Die Hard" was? Shoes that looked like feet. (So Bruce Willis could run through broken glass safely.) Now, every time I watch a Camaro turn into a giant bipedal robot, I get pissy if it doesn't look perfectly realistic in the proper lighting.[2]

We're in an escalating war against Suspension of Disbelief. We demand crazier and more visually stunning effects, and we demand that they be presented to us in such a way that we can stomach the greater disparity. Eventually, we're just going to become more desensitized and ask for *more, bigger* explosions in the next half-billion-dollar lens flare fire orgy. Sure, art pictures and romantic comedies will continue just as before, but the gap between "Blockbusters" and 'everything else' is going to keep getting wider as we discover we can make literally any thing we want appear on screen for cheaper and cheaper.

But hey, cool explosions, right?

---

[1] When she was a kid, five cents got her a couple cartoons, a movie, a newsreel, another movie, and popcorn. And they probably paid with the silver dollars her grandfather made in his basement.
[2] Or if it doesn't make the 'right' transforming sound.

OF LEGO, DISNEY AND POST-COLONIAL THEORY

The first LEGO set I ever owned was I think a little car with doors that swung out. I'm not counting Duplo or any of the other toys, just the genuine article. I think the second set, bought around the same time was a commercial airplane. It had wings and a little pilot and a baggage cart, and three little yellow boxes with doors each capable of holding maybe one 1x1 tall LEGO block. You could store these in the plane for transport by swinging the tail of the plane to one side with little red hinge pieces that were officially the coolest LEGO piece in existence at the time.[1] I still have mine on display on my bookshelf. Actually, I ended up combining these coolest pieces ever with the *next* coolest pieces ever: the Ice Planet Explorer set's mission commander with his orange laser buzz saw. And a sword. And the race car driver's opaque red helmet. And some blue epaulets. It's awesome.

I believe there was a point I was trying to make there and I'm fairly sure it was this: Pretty much every person reading this is at

Girlpants and Gasoline

least passingly familiar with the Dutch building toy. As soon as a child is old enough to start developing his or her motor coordination and the parents are reasonably certain s/he possesses the good sense not to immediately ingest the tiny, colorful bricks, that child is ushered into the wonderful world of tiny yellow people without knees.

Shockingly, I'm not even being hyperbolic with that statement. A few years ago I came across an ad placed by a man looking to buy LEGO sets for his son from any of the *Star Wars*, *Batman* or *Harry Potter* sets. At the time, I was looking to clean out my attic and unload two enormous storage containers of immaculately preserved *Star Wars* LEGOs, so the arrangement really just made itself. This guy paid good money for literally dozens of opened but complete and mostly mint LEGO sets. Why? Because he realized his son wasn't developing his fine motor coordination as quickly as he should have been. This incredible parent took to buying his kid "new" LEGO sets, dumping all the pieces on the floor and simply saying, "Pick them up." When his son would begin to paw at a pile of bricks, his father would stop him and gently tell him, "No, one at a time." After a year of this his son was building the tiny space ships and assorted periwinkle characters. That one transaction paid for six months of my car insurance and a year of this kid's birthday and Christmas gifts. Also, I won't lie, I completely held back on an X-Wing and the Millennium Falcon and built them that very day.

I think it was in the early nineties that things like police cruisers and tow trucks stopped being sufficiently interesting for imagination-based toys. Where was the flash, the excitement? The DayGlo colors kids saw on TV? More fantastic elements had to be ascribed to playsets. They just *had* to be. The alpine skier needed a glowing neon helmet and laser-chainsaw, because he was *an Ice Planet Explorer* with flying snowmobiles and bio domes. The fisherman became a *Deep Sea Exploration* technician, complete with giant octopus and ocean floor drilling habitat. Mechanics became *Space Colony Miners* riding rockets and churning out raw ore to collect their shiny, shiny crystals. And that's pretty much how the trend continues two decades later, though generously supported by the movie franchise playsets, now. The cops are still cops, I guess, but now they're *space cops!* Arresting *robots!* And *Aliens!*

Actually, there's something about those snarling, evil aliens in the few commercials I've seen that just emotes "lawlessness." Who are these vile creatures who would thwart the Yellow Man's benevolent rule of civilized space-ciety?

They're humanoid for the most part—we can start with that—in that the different species are bipedal, utilizing the same basic LEGO body and leg pieces as the Good Guy humans. However, they are also distinctly alien, featuring rather sinister head pieces. The 2009 "Space Police" line contained four original "evil alien" characters: a gray porcine/pachydermal man, a four-armed snarling insect, an amphibious thief who appears to be capable of 360° vision and who enjoys capes, and a skull-faced space biker with Lovecraftian mouth proboscises. Opposing these uncivilized, subhuman brutes exists the LEGO Space Police: two yellow[2] humans and what I am positive is a repaint of an android body from 1995.

Now ostensibly all this takes place in outer space. Since humans are not native to the vacuum of space the human members of Team Space Police have to wear their little helmets. The aliens, mind you, do not have helmets. In both commercials for the toy line, they can actually be seen floating through open space rather comfortably (though understandably a bit miffed at having been apprehended by their lawful masters). The logical conclusion then, in astrobiological terms, is that these creatures are evolutionarily suited for surviving in empty space, if only for short periods of time. This implies they evolved in and are native to a zero- or thin-atmosphere environment, very likely the asteroids/small inhospitable computer animated

Girlpants and Gasoline

moons that appear in LEGO's commercials.

From this we can assume that either:

a. these "aliens" are the rightful natural inhabitants of the rocks on which the Space Patrol has built its headquarters and penal colonies, or

b. they have, biologically, a certainly more valid right to be hanging around said asteroids.

But perhaps the Space Police arrived at the asteroid field and, seeing now modern structures or political/militaristic organization, claimed manifest destiny. How familiar would that be? A bunch of pale humans get together and go somewhere new to set up shop with all their pretty toys and enforce their laws irrespective of the local indigenous lifeforms. Hurray colonialism! Can we buy the Space Police "Cotton Field Harvest" playset, now? Maybe in a few years we can afford the Space Police "Civil Unrest" line, featuring one million little tiny LEGO men marching against discrimination of non-yellows. Perhaps it will come with little yellow attack dogs and fire hoses.

Edward Said, who regrettably passed away in 2003, was the preeminent authority on Post-Colonial theory. For those not familiar with modern literary criticism, the obscenely simplified gist of his work is that after a few hundred years Westerners felt bad about the whole 'conquering and oppressing everybody' thing and began to lavish praise upon native cultures for their differences and uniqueness. This became the ultra-chic thing to do among pretentious people, like spending a week in Nevada and "just abso*lute*ly falling in love with the native art[3]." This resulted in a corruption of actual foreign culture in the minds of Westerners, like getting that Aztec-y tapestry you hang over your sofa because a brown man outside Reno sold it to you and it cost $3 less than the wolf-howling-at-the-moon t-

David E. Zucker

shirt you had been eyeing.

Said was describing a fetishization by Western society of The Other, the "he who is not like the rest of us," something Said elucidated in his many papers on Exile Writings, Orientalism and Post-Colonial theory itself. Said saw experts of Western literature super-grouping Eastern cultures and traditions for the sake of discourse, but that oversimplification, misclassification and those improper perceptions inevitably created altered views of these cultures. This in turn, when put to paper in literature and textual studies, became considered historical canon, cyclically reinforcing wrongful beliefs among Western academics and further stereotyping members of global culture left absent from the discussion. Said saw the rise of The Other as a theoretical binary, something defined not by what it is, but what it *isn't*, in relation to something else and therefor dependent on that concept for any value. Said classified The Other as an intrinsically flawed binary to Western thought the same as Showalter discredited Second Stage feminist writing as a binary to traditionally male-centric writings.

Said didn't end the binary, though, so much as he encouraged Western scholars to look to the East for examples of alternative but equally valid traditions and cultures. Post-Colonialism has shaded quite a bit more than LEGO advertising in modern childhoods. Disney's *Aladdin* was an incredible movie adaptation of a great, truly legendary tale from the Middle East, featuring wonderful, up-beat and modern musical numbers and the rapid-fire voice acting of Robin Williams. Yet, observed carefully it is a decidedly slanted view of the story.

The title character, Aladdin, is a suave and witty young man possessing an American accent and rather Caucasian facial features for a sun-tanned Arabian street urchin. This is technically reasonable as the Middle East *is* and has been home to peoples of Mongoloid, Negroid *and* Caucasoid genealogies. Put simply, *there are plenty of*

Girlpants and Gasoline

white people in parts of the Middle East. Despite being somewhat more well-tanned than most Americans, Aladdin is an easily likable fellow, which is rather convenient for a hero.

Aladdin's nemesis Jafar, however, is imbued with distinctly anti-Christian, anti-Western symbolism for the purpose of making him a character easily *dislikable* by Western audiences. He has a lean, lanky frame and pencil-thin mustache reminiscent of Flash Gordon's Ming the Merciless. His wardrobe is black and red, stark and downright *pointy*. He wears an elaborate black turban and flowing Asiatic gowns. Additionally an evil wizard who employs talking animal familiars and a serpent motif, Jafar is a veritable menagerie of traits uncommon and uncouth to Western sensibilities, but familiarly Other and foreboding. He is recognizably alien and sinister where Aladdin is affable and relatable.

In the same vein, the sultanate of Agrabah employs royal guards who are comically shaped, inept and violent scimitar wavers, brutal in their execution of executions. The Sultan, meanwhile, is politically and literally tiny and insignificant, easily distracted or coerced and utterly oblivious to the vile machinations of his grand vizier. Though of lighter skin than the peasants of his land, the Sultan is walled off in his lavish palace of gardens and minarets, the beneficiary of royal lineage and feudal tax systems ripe for exploitation by British traders a few years down the line. His daughter Jasmine, meanwhile, is an honest, democratically, socially, progressively-minded young woman. It is her sense of logic and equality that convinced Aladdin to abandon his attempts to win her heart through, like Jaffar, magic and strict Islamic marriage law and to *actually* win her heart through bravery and fair treatment of the oppressed, freeing his own personal slave/genie. She is a testament to the wonder and civility of the British Colonial System, as well as the kindness, intelligence, and class it immediately bestowed upon subjugated brown people.

David E. Zucker

Consider again the little LEGO aliens: a grimacing mantis, a violent thing with dreadlocks and big lips; a greedy serpent and a slant-eyed barbarian. These sets are commodifications of The Other, literally selling to Westerners a fetishized version of what they perceive to be the opposite of themselves, snarling, dehumanized beasts uncaring and unfettered by puny human legal systems. In space.

Said postulated a more hopeful literary theory, Modernism, as a time when Western modes of thought are forced to recognize the validity of The Other not as a binary but as an equal alternative, a different but still legitimate worldview. Neither's mode of thought encompasses the entirety or even the fully "correct" view of complete human experience, but each a truthful part of the whole.

I dream of a world in which little LEGO boys and little LEGO alien girls can bathe in the same spring of little blue LEGO bricks. I dream of a world where there is no need for a LEGO Space Police force, because every LEGO being is imbued with love for that sacred gift of basic living LEGO dignity.

Also, everyone gets neon laser chainsaws.

---

[1] I have no way to verify this but, trust me, it was *awesome*.

[2] Read: "Caucasian." LEGO people are like *Simpsons* characters. A few minorities around to remind Whitey he's so much more enlightened these days.

[3] Or celebrities adopting babies from third-world nations, despite trite things like local adoption laws or the child having living parents. You know, stuff like that.

OF LAPSED JUDAISM

It's occurred to me just now that Sarah Silverman is really the only person attempting to make being Jewish sexy, and I'm pretty sure she's only doing it accidentally. (There's just something to saying you're meshuga for anal sex that drives a cantor wild.)

Today I've decided to make an effort to bring thick locks of glistening chest hair back into style. There's no reason open polyester and gold chains can't come back, even if disco never should. But how to do this? Frankly, it's still a hell of a lot funnier to make fun of Judaism than to praise it. So I figure we start small (like our penises) and work our way up from there.

The first step is to create a desire. I don't mean make us alluring, I mean the literal naming and popularization of the idea of wanting to have sex with a Jewish person. There was Jungle Fever, a strong desire to sleep with a black person. This led to a whole lot of urban kung-fu movies. More recently, Asiatic women have been spreading Yellow Fever as if it were actually malaria, chiefly through Fetish website and the Drive Fast Now! movie franchises. It has something to do with smooth, tanned skin, high cheek bones and frail, demure figures that have been socially trained to please their men through elaborate forms of rope bondage and cooking.

So now I introduce to you The Jew Flu.

"Oh man, do I want to hit that Sarah Silverman chick. I've got such a serious case of the Jew Flu for her. I'm gonna need some matzo ball soup STAT, bro! Can I afford the rise in my health insurance premiums if I submit a claim? Should I get a Roth IRA or invest my savings in long-term equity bonds for a guaranteed return at a later date? Oh, baby, baby, I'm meshuga for your shuga!"

See how wonderfully that works? It mystifies and alienates The Other while popularizing a sexualized stereotype in an alluring fashion. I almost went ahead with calling it the "Jewties," but found that a bit schoolyard for a euphemism for the desire to bang attractive Jewish people. Admittedly though, the idea of a "Jewtie shot" lends itself well to at least a few pick-up lines: "Hey, baby? Have you been inoculated? No? Well then I've got a little prick for you."

rimshot

NEVER FALL IN LOVE AT THE JERSEY SHORE

There are three different ways to witness a train wreck: be part of it, be next to it, or see it on the evening news. The gentleman inside the train is certainly in less than a desirable situation, but you can be absolutely certain he will point to it as one of the most life-altering, pivotal moments in his existence. Onlookers can experience the sight firsthand, and while that experience may not be as acute as someone who nearly died taking part in the crash, they probably had a much broader view of the situation from their removed vantage point. They can probably tell you what led to the bloodshed, how it looked as it happened, and how people carried themselves after, but this will always be an outside perspective.

The only other way to see a train wreck is to hear about it after the debacle has been more or less sorted out, the dead counted, the investigation begun, and the blood either washed away or strate-gically left within camera shot as an emotional symbol to the families at home. This is also how MTV makes its money.

David E. Zucker

I spent three years watching *Jersey Shore* after I decided it was awful, yet still somehow sociologically fascinating. I watched Season 1 out of the same morbid curiosity everyone else had, albeit a bit more like Jane Goodall than I imagine most others did. By the start of Season 2 I was taking notes on what appeared to be thematic points left either by surreptitious MTV editors or, I hoped, by simple human interaction adhering to a legitimate societal moral compass. I was assured[1] that after season *three* the show would end and I would find my central premise for the show, see the end of the story arc, as it were. So I waited.

Then MTV paid the Italian government enough money to lift the cast's collective and individual bans on ever entering the country.

Season 4 will probably be labeled as one of the worst in the show's run, if not *the* worst, the only competition it has being Season 2, which was thematically "off" only in that the cast had a sense of what they were supposed to do and a vague notion that they were going to be at least minor celebrities. It was a transition from what the show was originally billed as ("*The Real World: Jersey* Shore"), to the show it eventually became. Season 4 was just the made-for-TV movie of the show's run. *Saved By the Bell* had its *College Years* and *New Class* to milk the franchise dry, but the stand-alone movie *Hawaii Style*, followed the 'Summer Special' mentality of "lets send the cast to an exotic location and watch the hijinks."

Jersey Shore Season 4 suffered from similar problems. Angelina,[2] the only cast member to have been kicked off the show—*twice* in fact–had been officially replaced with Deena, Snooki's supposed friend and co-meatball a season earlier. (This followed standard sit-com procedure for introducing a new, cuter child when the previous youngest was no longer precocious enough.) The re-maining cast was then reunited and flown to Italy under the loose premise of introducing Vinny to his distant relatives. Housemates alternated between being immensely into their own shit, and being generally as bewildered by their predicament as they were in Season

Girlpants and Gasoline

1, and the audience has been for the previous three straight seasons. Effectively, Season 4 did nothing but bridge the gap between "Woo, we're kind of a big deal, but it's over," and "You can't get rid of us, we're too big." It is notable only in that it reunited Ronnie and Sam as a functional couple, and can retroactively be said to portray The Situation's increasingly erratic behavior due to abuse of prescription pain killers.

It was then a big deal for Season 5 to be advertised as the official end to *Jersey Shore*. Somewhere, a far-sighted executive saw that the show was approaching the point where it was less profitable to keep paying the housemates than to put on a big todo of ending it and then recycling the idea a thousandfold over the next several years of programming. Season 5 is, without a doubt, the *College Years* of the series. Its daily plots are more obviously forced, background characters like Jenny's long-term boyfriend Roger and Snooki's beau Jionni become more prominent, and there's an effort made on the part of the showrunners and editors to thematically close certain relationships and running themes. It was important to tie up the questions fans had been asking.

Allow that to register a moment. It became *necessary* to 'massage' a reality show until it came to the conclusion expected of it.

If all of the show is looked back on as a whole, with clear delineation between Seasons 1-3, and Seasons 4-5, *Jersey Shore* is and always has been ... a love story.

The Couple, fairly obviously, was Ronnie Ortiz-Magro and Samantha Giancola. Ron and Sam met on the show and dissolved their relationship *at the reunion show*, reunited in Season 2 and then imploded, reuniting yet again during Season 3, whereby they fell into what I will call, as I believe Pauly-D referred to on several occasions, a "shitstorm." For the short version: Sam was insecure and Ron was something of a dick to her, until a turning point in Season 3 where it became apparent that Sam actually had deeply routed abandonment

David E. Zucker

and trust issues which directly fed into Ron's desire to act out in retribution. Somewhere, *Ron* became the sympathetic character, because all he wanted to do was love the girl he loved without being daily put into positions where he couldn't express himself and ended up hurting her. It was a sad story, but it was the obvious and best decision when the two agreed to permanently end their relationship. Ron says it "was never real," yet it "destroyed our time in the house." If you go back all the way to episode 1, the very first introduction to Ronnie is his voice over footage of him packing for the Shore House, saying the one rule he openly lamented breaking three seasons later; "I have one rule: never fall in love at the Jersey shore."

It was brilliantly farsighted of the Season 1 editor to make that Ronnie's introduction, knowing he and Sam would eventually hook up, but that it worked out so poignantly for the entire run of the show's five season was a combination of blind luck and, well, the demands of society. Let us assume, going into Season 1 Episode 1, all the housemates understood that sex, amongst themselves and with outsiders, was tacitly encouraged. (Mind you, *The Real World* was in its seventeenth season at this point, well within the zeitgeist.) The male housemates in fact discuss their prospects while waiting for the first female cast members to arrive, so let's take that assumption as fact. Ron's rule was, in context, more about normal behavior while vacationing in Seaside Heights: "My only rule: never fall in love at the Jersey Shore. *Never*. Ever ever ever....I mean I don't really know what love means. The whole thing about this is getting laid. You pretty much take your shirt off and they come to you. It's like a fly comes to shit." Don Juan he ain't, but perceptive, maybe. The principal goal of *Jersey Shore* was never to help two twenty-somethings of sub-average intelligence[3] find love. It was about taking the crazy Party Girl from every past reality program and putting them under one roof during Summer Vacation to film the ensuing chaos.

Then America fell in love with Ron and Sam. The relationship

Girlpants and Gasoline

wasn't allowed to stay dead. They were happy, but *we* knew there was secret footage Ron hadn't seen, vilifying Sammie's hypocrisy. They broke up because of it. Then we demanded they be housed together a second Summer. And then again. And when Romeo and Juliet lay poisoned and stabbed and the whole bloody affair was done with at Season 3's close, we flew them to one of the most romantic locales on Earth to bring that corpse back on life support. And they fought, and they fucked, and then they were happy at last.

And it was boring. Season 5 was a giant close-out of issues pertaining to these distinct characters and reality shows as a whole. It was the epilogue to a train wreck, the part where the reporter goes in and asks the little girl with the maimed leg *how it feels*. Ronnie and Sam were happy for almost the entire season. She was less passive-aggressive and paranoid, he was less douchey and more openly committed to her alone. The show lost its A-plot. B-stories ruled the season, Snooki and Jionni and to a lesser extent Jenni and Roger were made out to be the crazy couples, but everyone knew the Big Game was over.

Jersey Shore was an exercise in controlled relational eugenics. We paired off a bunch of spray-tanned pandas, locked them in a zoo, and went bonkers when two of them started mating. And even when they didn't get along we pushed and prodded those pandas into miserably sharing their lives together until it changed who they were at their very centers. Damned if they didn't find a way out anyway.

Jersey Shore was a show about love. Its manufacturing, its forcing, and its controlling … but ultimately just love.

---

[1] By a professional source I became acquainted with in the production company. Full disclosure: I temped as a P.A. during the shooting of *FriendZone*'s pilot season to help out a friend. I was also in an episode of Kevin Smith and AMC's *Comic Book Men*, but that is pure bragging and completely irrelevant.

[2] Amusingly, Angelina made a paid appearance at an Asian fusion restaurant/bar near

my house that year, while pregnant. Paying the girl who makes poor decisions to be at a bar seemed in-character.

[3] Actually, Sam majored in sociology before joining the *Jersey Shore* cast. Ron worked with his father in real estate, Mike *was* a personal trainer, Pauly-D a DJ, Angelina a waitress, Snooki (an adopted Chilean, as a tan-related factoid) studied to be a *veterinary technician*, Jenny (Spanish-Irish, so fully 25% of the cast wasn't even Italian) had her own graphic design company and a blackbelt, and Vinny by his own account graduated a semester early with a 3.9 GPA in political science, had been an aid to a New York assemblyman, and took the LSAT the day *Jersey Shore* premiered. Law School was his *backup* plan. Proof, I suppose, that television really *does* rot your brain, whether you're in front of the camera or behind it.

ON 'HOT CHICKS'

My friends have raised an interesting question: "Where the Hell do hot chicks go in the Winter?" Do they just *disappear*? They certainly don't go to the Jersey Shore. And how is it that as soon as the weather turns even remotely nice, they instantly appear wearing booty shorts? Is it magic? Are they familiars to a cabal of secret *wizards*?

They may be facetious[1] but they're not *wrong*. When the weather turns cold, attractive girls just seem to recede into their parkas. Men subsist on t-shirts and the occasional polo all year long, so by the time Spring rolls around and we're thinking about breaking out baseball because there hasn't been anything to catch our attentions for four months, *BAM!* That's when the sluts reappear.

Oh god, did I really type that? No, they're not sluts. Well, not most of them, at least. I'm sure there are a few actual sluts in the whole, but they're less responsible for giving everyone else that bad name than men are. That actually brings me back to my original

David E. Zucker

point, which is this: Men are oblivious, entitled assholes, and women have been trained to either buck the patriarchy and live a life of hardship, or when possible buy into the controlling system and play their role to their own maximum benefit. In Winter, after such a dearth of bare skin and toned shoulders, public locations become suddenly inundated with every even remotely attractive woman jumping at the chance to show off whatever it is she's priming for beach season.

Gender studies aside, we *know* some of these women. Maybe not you or me personally, but *someone* somewhere must know them and know where they go in the Winter. They don't transform into grotesque monsters like Dr. Jekyll that first chilly week in October. They have to *go* somewhere. So this is my theory:

Hot chicks are like bears.

Yes, you can make some type of "they're cool to look at but stand next to one and you'll just yammer and stammer and wet yourself in terror and then run away" analogy, or, sure, you could equate her friends to a she-bear's little cubs and realize that to in any way get near them will result in Momma Bear going completely feral and mauling you into a bloody stump that was once a man. You could, really.

But here's the honest truth: **attractive women hibernate**. Every Fall the gorgeous girl you mooned over all Summer returns to school or work or wherever it is she spends the part of her life that isn't a vacation, and she prepares for the Winter months.

If she is in college she puts on what is called the "Freshman Fifteen"–approximately seven kilos of pure Hot Pocket–and wraps herself in a warm bed, surrounding herself with blankets, snacks, multiple seasons of "progressive" women's television shows and possibly an ill-conceived Walmart beta fish that will die within six weeks. The few times that she does wander out of her nest in Winter,

Girlpants and Gasoline

it will be grudgingly, angrily and hungrily, lashing out at those around her and fighting openly for even the most meager scrap of high-protein sustenance.

Towards the tail-end of Winter, Hot Girl will begin to stir in her hovel, the last episodes of her *Carrie Diaries* boxed set drawing to a close without the one perfect kiss between the chisel-jawed mop-top and the chisel-faced titular blonde twig. She will slowly start to spend more time outside of her cave interacting with other creatures, even beginning to take physical care of herself again. She will refuse to be seen looking like a "loser" in over-sized hoodies and track pants, unshowered and unkempt. Eventually–and usually secretly–she will begin the arduous process of "getting ready for the beach," which is actually a bizarre ritual comprised of poorly-executed remedial components of yoga, aerobics, cardio and awkward grunting/lamenting, followed by a massive calorie burn achieved through all the complaining she'll do about not being able to eat [substance-X] anymore.

However all of this is apparently worth it to her, as come the first sunny day of Spring, Hot Chick will shed her outer layers of gosling-down pillow puff jacket and sloganized-butt sweat pants for a pink spaghetti tank and a pair of sloganized-butt short-shorts. Who wears short shorts? Externally validated women wear short shorts. But that's fine. Hot Chick is not a 'slut.'

What she is doing is called "peacocking," or "presenting," in the animal kingdom.[2] She is showing off absolutely all the goods at once, putting the milk up on the auction block to see who is interested in buying a cow. She only *looks* like a slut because she craves your *attention* like a slut. If she were doing this all Winter, the other hot chicks would excommunicate her sluttish ass for making the rest of the pack look bad, but this is a social display designed to attract a *mate*. There is actually no promiscuity involved. Hot Chick is very selective when it comes to finally selecting a male to accompany back to his cave (hers is likely still in disarray).[3]

David E. Zucker

Prairie-dogging like Punxsutawney Phil from their burrows of sloth and unattractiveness, attractive women come out in Spring to find love, or at least procreate and replenish the species. It's a brief window of opportunity to flaunt some plumage and snag a desirable gene pool. If there are no jerks around, they might not see their shadows and hide away again.

Either that or they all migrate South or something. Like geese. Maybe hot chicks are like geese.

---

[1] And certainly chauvinistic in their phrasing

[2] And in PUA (Pick-Up Artist) culture. Males are just as guilty of this as bimbos and bison.

[3] These are the precise circumstances that create "slut shaming," degradation of women for apparent promiscuity devoid of fact, likely resultant from the discrepancy between a man's perception of her sexuality and her refusal to acquiesce to his advances.

PRETTY FUNNY (FOR A GIRL)

According to industry legend, comedy was first discovered in 1564 with the serendipitous exchange "How many Puritans does it take to change the candle in a reading lamp?"/"None; they won't touch anything that looks like a dick." Soon the joke evolved such that the suffix '[x] is dick-like' was dropped entirely and merely became implied. For example: "Why did the chicken cross the road?"/"To get to the other side, [you dick]." This naturally progressed to the simple conclusion that if one did not get the joke, one was likely to be a dick oneself. If a joke failed spectacularly, meanwhile, listeners were encouraged to make the comic aware of his own dick-like behavior, often with the phrase, "Boo!...Dick!" Thus heckling was also born. This is important to note, as prior to the innovation of heckling it was simply customary to behead the unfunny. Anne Boleyn for example, the first comedienne, following a terrifically poor routine about the difference between manservants and ladies-in-waiting, was summarily executed, setting back the cause of female comedy performers decades, at least until Catherine the Great did some really amazing material with a horse.

This is where we enter, a world where comediennes seem cursed to either tell the same, traditionally phallus-centric jokes men

David E. Zucker

tell or, well, suck. Why? What is it that makes the possession of ovaries somehow antithetical to being funny? Is it that women's issues are simply not topically funny, or is there something in the performers themselves that detracts from the essence of their acts? (Boobs?) I refuse to believe the assertion, "Women just aren't funny." I have *met* women[1]. True, many of them are not funny, but no more than the number of *men* who aren't funny either. It is not like there is a series of chemical encodings on the Y-chromosome that endows in a person the ability to accurately guesstimate how many [x]es it takes to screw in a lightbulb.

At the time of this writing, the preeminent comedienne in terms of success and name recognition is unarguably Sarah Silverman. Why is Sarah Silverman funny? Is it because she is an attainably attractive woman in the traditionally old-boys' club that is late night comedy programming who subverts expectations and breaks out of the shell society has built for a young Jewish woman?

No, not really. It's that she is an attainably attractive, seemingly relaxed woman who tells dick-and-fart jokes with the kind of language that would make grown men blush. If she had planned this, it would be a great dichotomy, some kind of grand juxtaposition by which to push forward the cause of breaking societal perceptions of femininity. Maybe it still is, but Silverman won't cop to it just yet.

"My dad thought it was funny to teach us to swear," Silverman told *Playboy* in 2002. "He thought it was hilarious. I was the innocent vessel through which he was able to say anything." In the same article she disavows, despite her own act, that she does *not* partake in bukkake films, anal sex or any of the other fun activities she mentions, though she does occasionally wet the bed. Delightful.

Certainly, she seems the type to unabashedly voice her opinion. Aside from achieving every young Jewish girl's dream of making Daddy happy, Sarah Silverman's success seems to be based on appearing the exact opposite of a "nice little girl," acting as

Girlpants and Gasoline

aggressively chauvinistic and frequently disgusting as possible.

Juxtaposing masculine crassness with traditional images of femininity is also the calling card of stand-up comedy's "Queen of Mean," Lisa Lamponelli, an insult comic whose only peers are Don Rickles and a stogy-smoking latex dog puppet. Her schtick is arriving on stage dressed like Suzy Homemaker, in a poodle skirt or floral housedress and pearls with a Mary Tyler Moore haircut. Harkening back to the days of "Leave It to Beaver," where social controversy consisted of having the colored milkman reprimand the white children, Miss Lamponelli then proceeds to fling the most racist, sexist, and classless language at anyone close enough to take the hit. Again, anal sex, dicks, and bodily fluids dominate her set, though in a heavier concentration than Silverman.[2]

Is there a saving grace? Yes. While Silverman makes herself into something of a sex object as she performs, Lamponelli's act is designed to do this with gusto. She degrades herself more than anyone (and everyone) in the audience, but retains her dignity in some small way. By taking with a smile her own most vile abuse, Lamponelli takes some of the sting from her outward attacks. Not only does it prevent anyone *else* from making the same attacks, but it diffuses any notion that she may actually be a bigot.

More poignantly, in dressing to meet a vintage, hyper-stylized ideal of Americana, Lamponelli provides an abstracted backdrop of traditional femininity to her most destructive, hurtful, and decidedly masculine routines. Lamponelli reminds us that women can tell the same jokes as men while not necessarily playing the fool. It can be done intelligently and in a pretty dress, thereby illustrating gender equality in that women can retain their own identity while engaging in a traditionally male gender role.

Elaine Showalter argued of Feminist criticism that it tends toward tunnel-vision, basing everything on the assumption that,

David E. Zucker

though women are morally equal to men, intrinsically the two genders are diametrically opposed. Men are the hunters, women the gatherers; men are the warriors and defenders, women the nurturers.

This kind of thinking establishes Feminism as a critical binary, entirely dependent for its definition on the same gender separatism it rails against. It marks Feminism not by what it *is* on its face, but by that which it *is* not, an absence or a "lack" of masculinity. By *opposing,* Feminism can only describe itself by equally *validating* masculism.

Sarah Silverman is novel because she is a woman telling men's jokes. Lisa Lamponelli because she tries to force the two together and feed off the socially tectonic stress. But this still presupposes that much of comedy is in the exclusive domain of men, masculine behavior which, at its core, is ridicule of the self and others. It is competitive, it is violent and it wreaks of testosterone more than a giant naked Roman wrestling match that is totally and completely, one hundred percent *not* gay[3]. Could the more crass, masculine elements of stand-up be removed from the equation and still produce comedy?

There is an incredibly talented stand-up comic by the name of Maria Bamford, whose diminutive voice and image contrast astute, decidedly not-falsetto observations and spot-on impersonations of those close to her. This talent has netted her a CD, two cable Television specials, a headlining slot with Patton Oswalt and Brian Posehn on the "Comedians of Comedy Tour" and its associated TV series, and even a set of Christmas commercials for Target where she is dual-cast as decoration-obsessed twin sisters. She also has numerous voice acting credits. Bamford's material is original, fresh and religiously rehearsed. Her situational comedy features traditionally feminine issues, locales, and is almost entirely devoid of any male presence. Unlike Silverman or Lamponelli, Bamford does not rely on her femininity being in opposition to anything except her own perpetually-prepubescent frame. Also unlike Silverman and Lamponelli,

Girlpants and Gasoline

despite her numerous performing credits and twenty years in stand-up, Bamford is not a household name.

This was Showalter's concern, that removing everything that is even remotely masculine leaves Feminism lacking and flat. Bamford is incredibly amusing. I love watching her specials, but the majority of her act relies on the idea that her natural voice is high and childlike, while her personal style is not indicative of traditional femininity. There is the same pressure to be "womanly," but no masculine force to play off or model femininity against. Bamford's act raises the question "What *is* feminine?" but without providing an answer.

Silverman and Lamponelli, then Bamford represent to comedy what in *Toward a Feminine Poetics* Elaine Showalter described as the first two stages of Women's Literature. Women like Silverman and Lamponelli attempt to equal men by rivalry, internalizing their differences as assumed by men. This works, for a time, but perpetuates the false differences between men and women that were already the problem. Women like Bamford then reject these assumed traits and roles, but in doing so leave themselves a very narrow range of experience to draw from, that which is exclusive to women's life experiences but not already co-opted by male comedians.

Showalter believed that starting around 1920 Women's Literature moved out of its secondary "Feminist" stage and into a modern "Female" phase. The goal became to define Women's Literature not solely in opposition to traditional works, but to explore the vast "wilderness" of feminine writing, work that looked at the *universal* human experience through the lens of being a woman. Women's writing should not be an entirely separate language, then, but merely the same language in a different accent. This is what Bamford is shooting for, but in ill proportion. By focussing on making the condition of exclusively being a woman funnier, one part of the audience is still being elevated over another, and an inequality persists.

David E. Zucker

As far as literary criticism goes, this works. It's ideal, in fact. Much work will continue to have a masculine bent but there will also be a fair amount of work knowingly designed to study from a female vantage. The vast majority of scholarly discussion, then, would come from a learned majority knowingly incorporating both considerations into a universally human view of a text. By this same model, comedy should be *universally* funny, utilizing a comedienne's status as a woman only to fuel certain jokes and broaden her audience to both men and women. The same would apply to a male comic occasionally going "blue" so long as it does not detract from the greater scheme of the bit. The joke teller's sex, again ideally, should be incidental.

This is something we're actually beginning to see more of. Humorists like Sloane Crosley are seeking a window of literary existence that is neutrally feminine. Each essay in her semi-autobiographical collection *I Was Told There'd Be Cake* is witty and self-deprecating. However her prose would remain hilarious even if one were to completely annihilate pronouns from her book like a redaction-happy Tarzan. The fact that she is a woman is superfluous to Crosley's humor. Sure, it might be slightly more unsettling if a *man* were keeping a drawer full of plastic shame ponies, but the joke really isn't the horses, it's constantly and without provocation receiving the same bizarre gift from significant others, then keeping them in a dark drawer like *memento mori* of relationships passed. It is an odd but entirely recognizable quirk everyone is susceptible to. Everyone has a shame drawer. Or box or back of the closet. Few people possess ponies.

Yet what is the point[4] in having a conversation about funny women without discussing Tina Fey? Tina Fey: Tamer of the Jimmy Fallon, Sweater Aficionado and the only person to ever write a Lindsey Lohan movie that can be watched without turning off the

Girlpants and Gasoline

sound. What can really be said here of Tina Fey that hasn't already been written across the bathroom walls at 30 Rockefeller Plaza?

Fey is a woman, as far as I can tell, and I believe I saw in a Discover Card ad that she has a small child of some sort. Or possibly a pomeranian. However, Fey might also be the only person on network television who understands how to properly develop a significantly female voice without alienating a predominantly male prime-time audience.

Watch the first five minutes of *30 Rock*'s pilot episode and you can see that Fey's character hates *anyone* who cheats. She is a *non-discriminating* hater. Fey's comedy style is to illustrate ridiculousness of situations and behavioral hilarity that isn't dependent on gender, but personality type. Jack Donaghy is a man's man. Tracy Jordan and Jenna Maroney are a postmodern farce of race- and gender-based comedy. Liz Lemon may be a neurotic doormat, but she is also the closest semblance to an intelligent observer on the show.

And yet all of these characters spring from Fey's design. She herself only plays out a fraction of her material. Liz Lemon may be a woman when a woman is needed for the show, but Fey's humor is far broader, encompassing the zany antics of all her characters, both male and female. *Everyone* is borderline clinically *psychotic*. *Everyone* is a self-destructive ass. That's funny.

This is the heart of things: human beings waste an inordinate amount of time hating each other for being the wrong shade of brown or for possessing the wrong secondary sex characteristics. It makes no sense at all to hate people for their physical differences when we could just as easily be hating people for *who they are on the inside*.

Do not assume that a woman isn't funny simply because she is a woman. There may be many, much more interesting reasons why she isn't funny, and very few of those probably have anything to do with her vagina.

David E. Zucker

---

[1] Shut up, you don't *know* that I haven't.

[2] In one televised special, Lamponelli spends a fair portion of her stage time regarding a nice interracial gay couple, who very charmingly accept her racist dick jokes about gay butt sex. It's her insult comedy hat-trick.

[3] Alright, maybe it's *a little* gay.

[4] Read: "profitability."

On Women's Shoes

I am about to improve your chances with attractive women exponentially:

Granting that it is mediated by her individual personality, but in almost all cases the more beautiful a woman is, the more she hates her feet.

This is actually pretty understandable. Feet are, after all, pretty weird. Big fleshy trapezoids are what they are. What are they *doing* down there? How do the *work*? Juggalo-grade miracles all up in there.

But look at the logic in play: the more beautiful a girl is the fewer physical traits she *has* to complain about. No civilized culture valuing modesty would allow a woman to walk around actually *thinking* herself a Venusian goddess. All her friends would hate her for being such a shallow, conceded bitch. At the same time, until a woman achieves that a level of complete, bitchy hotness, she psychologically *needs* to find something awful in her appearance. It's what keeps her in line, keeps her from being completely unlikeable, even something towards which she can work at bettering. It's an equilibrium of attractiveness, ensuring all attractive women maintain a mentally 'healthy' level of body dysmorphia. Sure, there are calves and earlobes and other weird body parts women can easily latch onto to prove to herself how hideous she must be, but feet are just weird enough to become an easy target, and if it's not the feet it's something even sillier, even more vehemently.

1. The more attractive the woman, the fewer unattractive physical traits.
2. Feet are always weird.

∴. A woman can always fall back on hating her feet.

Here is where things become exciting: as an attractive woman more closely approaches the self-realization that she is disgustingly attractive, that tipping point between giving up and becoming an 'egotistical bitch' or accepting her small imperfections as natural and beautiful in their own way, she comes to rely on loathing her feet all the more.

Now consider women's shoes. They are the opposite of feet; they are designed to be *cute*. Subtle curves and color-coordination, they are the Platonic ideal of a foot designed for form in place of function. The right shoes can make or break the perfect outfit: any black top may do, but shoes *need* to compensate for the foot's innate lack of appeal. The shoes *need* to be right.

Men, never question your lady's shoes.

However, if you're a pick-up artist/jerk trying to find an 'in' with an attractive lady, I might suggest aiming a gentle neg at her feet. Try to work in an off-handed Daddy Issues comment at the same time. I'm sure that'll work wonders.

"SMILE WHEN YOU SAY THAT"

A COMPREHENSIVE ANALYSIS OF MODERN AMERICAN STAND-UP COMEDY BY PRINCIPLE ASPECT UTILIZING UNNECESSARILY LONG SUBTITLES WHICH PROVIDE EXPOSITION YOU'LL LIKELY ENCOUNTER IN A FEW SECONDS ANYWAY

My grandmother used to explain Yiddish to me like so: "A *schmegegge* is the one who *spills* the soup; a *schlemiel* is the one the soup spills *on*.[1]" Considering, however, that the last comedian she saw was likely Danny Kaye at The Copa, I'm reasonably certain Grandma wasn't trying eek out an explanation for the entirety of modern American comedy.

Still, the analogy holds up well. Certain people will simply be funny because they make hilarity happen. They will have talent and wit, maybe even a little (read: "heaps of") luck in going about it and they will likely spend long hours practicing time-honored techniques like purposefully stepping on a rake or injuring their reproductive organs. Other people, unfortunately for them, will only be funny by the sheer chance of accident. They can only hope to harness for comedic benefit the awesome natural forces at play when life decides to injure them in their reproductive organs.

Yet all this talk of gonad injuries raises another question: "What *is* funny?" This spurs more: Is it situational? Conversational? Impersonational? Do you say funny *things* or do you *say* things funny? Who is on first and what exactly *is* the deal with airline food, anyway? We can only ever hope to answer these questions by examining *how* certain modes of comedy work for individual comedians. From this it might be possible to tease out notions of how certain concepts or behaviors take on seemingly inherent, laughable qualities.

We have to begin asking ourselves the same question all young comedians come to ask themselves: *What is the most important thing in comedy?*

Girlpants and Gasoline

David E. Zucker

Girlpants and Gasoline

"Timing."

David E. Zucker

What is funny?

Carol Burnett said, "Comedy is tragedy plus time." Gilbert Gottfried famously recovered from near career suicide after making a 9/11 joke only three weeks after the attacks. *South Park* decided AIDS should finally be considered funny after exactly 22.3 years. Something awful has happened, yes, but its impact *on the audience* has weakened over time, enough so that it now finds it acceptable to laugh at another's pain.

There's an adage that all comedy is laughter at another's misfortune.[2] Adults laugh at stupid young people, young people laugh at senile old farts, old farts laugh at ethnic minorities. There's always someone a few degrees far enough removed that their pain can amuse you. It may not be funny to laugh at a fat, borderline autistic kid falling down, but Winnie the Pooh getting stuck in a rabbit hole is goddam hilarious.

How is funny?

Taking derision as the subject matter, time, then, is the method. A good joke ends with the unexpected. It leads the listener to a logical conclusion and then turns it on its head in such a way as to leave you feeling foolish for not getting their first. *Timing* is the element to give a joke its gusto. To hit a punchline too early lessens its impact; to wait too long distances it from the setup.

Most comedians tend toward blending subject matter and their own performance style, meshing original content with time-tested models for *how* they tell the joke. This considered, every comedic style can now be described as a balance of Subject ("saying funny things") and Form ("saying things funny").

Girlpants and Gasoline

Stand-Up

There is perhaps nothing more terrifying in professional comedy than stand-up. You, alone, displayed on stage in front of a dimly-lit sea of blank faces, delivering your own material with only the modest ability you've achieved through countless hours of re-hearsal, praying to some higher power that when you come to a punchline the audience is willing to laugh instead of tearing a gaping hole through your chest with their shining spotlights and gut-wrench-ing silence. Of course, if you can master timing and adopt an almost a conversational tone, then it's all gravy.

You just need to determine if your material can stand on its own. If it can, you'll likely be a situational comic or a story teller, someone who talks about things that are funny. If you realize the majority of your act is not at all very good and requires a metric tonne of ridiculous voices and yelling to prevent the audience from noticing, well, then you're probably Dane Cook.

Sounding funny isn't by necessity a low-brow method of comedy. Impersonators like Frank Caliendo, Pablo Fransisco or Gabriel Igelsias all depend heavily on *sounding* a certain way, but at their core the bits are still comprised of good, solid material: people, places, situations, and a resolution.

Likewise, there are many comedians who lean heavily on sounding funny to emphasize a more absurd humor. Mitch Hedberg, God rest him, ran on 80% style, 4% subject and 16% illicit narcotics. The late Hedberg comprised his act mostly of one-line parapros-dokians[3] and longer stories comprised of interconnected wordplay. Constantly battling stage fright, Hedberg developed a performance style that played up his awkward delivery and self-criticism. While recording of his first album, *Strategic Grill Locations*, Hedberg seemingly made the audience laugh so hard he cracked up at himself. When a lull finally set in, Hedberg stretched out the uncomfortable chuckle saying, "Yeah, you thought I was laughing there, but really, I didn't have an end to the joke." Consider that for a moment: Mitch Hedberg is so good at telling jokes *he doesn't even need a punchline*. The way Hedberg performed, the comedy wasn't created entirely by the substance of the joke, but primarily by the timing and nature of the delivery. The audience became a single awkward giggle, waiting for a punchline they knew they could never fully anticipate.

A wonderfully tragic example of relying too heavily on sounding funny, Mr. Cook is best known for shouting, flailing wildly and frequently using basic stage elements in pantomiming his act, all while wearing $300 jeans and a children's medium t-shirt. Despite his financial success and notoriety, Cook has endured fierce criticism by the public and other comedians, notably from 2006 allegations over stealing material from acts by Joe Rogan and Louis C.K.[4]

Probably the worst criticism is that he simply is not funny. In a 2006 interview with online magazine Bullz-Eye, *Blue Collar Comedy Tour* veteran Ron White said Dane Cook "does not make me laugh, at all, in any way, shape or form." Two years later comedian Nick DiPaolo likewise told *The Howard Stern Show*, "He doesn't make me laugh." However DiPaolo grants Cook a deeper understanding, adding, "But that doesn't mean he's not funny."

Flip on one of his stand-up specials and you'll have to admit Dane Cook is fun to watch[5]. The energy he puts out, the screaming and sweating and jumping, that all creates an excitement around him. Dane Cook can talk about always wanting to kick down a door or own a monkey, but what he's always driving at is *everyone thinks the things he thinks*. Cook's hook is hitting on so many rememberable topics so quickly and so close together that it lights a spark of recognition in the audience and validates the ideas others thought were dumb when they first thought them. 'He's saying what we've all been thinking!'

Even Ron White had to agree Cook's performance style is

Girlpants and Gasoline

successful. In the same Bullz-Eye interview, White conceded, "It looks like smoke and mirrors. But it works for him." However much of a douchebag Cook may appear, one has to respect the fact that Cook's model can be made to make *anything* seem funny. Gesticulate wildly enough, validate how as a child everyone wanted to travel through space or some equally universal thought, and Dane Cook makes another small fortune. The only legitimate critique of Dane Cook is that he uses the form of *saying things funny* to completely skirt the issue of having to come up with originally funny material. And if David Blaine can out-magic David Copperfield by camping out in an ice block for a week, why shouldn't the most wildly successful comedian of the last decade be a comic who doesn't say anything that's particularly funny?

---

[1] Anyone familiar with "Laverne and Shirley" may also recall from the opening theme song a *schlimazel,* which would be a synonym for *schmegegge.* Yiddish is actually quite the diverse language when it comes to complaining.

[2] The German *Schadenfreude* is trussed up as a catch-all term for this malicious delight, purportedly having no English equivalent. This is however false. The Greek-rooted "epicaricacy" has simply fallen out of use since the 18th century. Feel free to use that the next time you're stuck making smalltalk at a party with pretentious asshats. Also, feel free to add, "Suck it! You just got OED'd!" at the end. Maybe throw up a hashtag.

[3] A statement whose second half causes you to go back and reevaluate the first. (I had to look it up, too.)

[4] Let's be honest, some of them were pretty common ideas, but if you're really stealing from Joe Rogan you've hit rock bottom.

[5] I know you still have a CD somewhere. It was practically required listening for any group of suburban youths back in the middle 'oughts. You can't even sell those things back at the mall, they're so common.

ON AVOCADOS

Every time I put an avocado back in the "FRUIT" bin of my refrigerator, the tomatoes stare at me accusingly. I don't know why I feel the need to cave to societal pressure and leave my tomatoes in the "VEGETABLE" bin; all I know is they've got to be pretty mad by this point.

Botanically speaking, there is no such thing as a "vegetable." A plant has roots, stems, leaves, flowers and fruit, but biologically there just isn't a part of a plant you can point at and say, "Vegetable." Potatoes and other tubers are fat roots, asparagus is predominantly stem with a bit of leaf up at the top, lettuce is mostly leaf.

Tomatoes are seeded fruits, protecting the tomato plant's gene pool in a nutritious casing of tomato-y meat. Apples too, are a fruit, as are oranges and mangos and lemons, limes, kiwis, strawberries, lychee nuts, cantaloupe, tangelos and the cape gooseberry. Every fruit we put in the "FRUIT" drawer is a fruit. Yet the "VEGETABLE" drawer is a willy-nilly hodgepodge of shoddy horticulture.

Girlpants and Gasoline

I've tried redefining the drawers: "Things I Would Not Put on a Sandwich;" "Things Which Classically Top A Salad;" "Foods I Do Not Want To Taste Before Noon;" nothing seems to stick. I blame the avocados, mostly. At this point, I am inclined to believe that the bins of my refrigerator are separated into "SWEET TASTING FRUITS" and "BLAND THINGS."

That still leaves me a bit unsure of where the avocados belong, but since I can only find room for them in the "FRUIT" bin, I at least don't feel like I owe anyone an apology.

THE DEATH THROES OF PRINT MEDIA:

WEBCOMICS AS A CREATIVE COMMUNITY

Scott McCloud, creator of long-running comic series *Zot!*, in his 2000 graphic analysis of the comics industry *Reinventing Comics* postulated that restrictions and limitations resulting from current methods of comics production stifled both the creativity and the profitability of the industry. In fairness to "The Industry," *Reinventing Comics* was McCloud's *second* trade comic book detailing the death of print comic media.

However anachronistic that may be, in expressing his qualms with comics' then-current modes of production, McCloud touted the internet as a likely source for the growth and expansion, both for comics' form and content. Believing *digital delivery* of comics to be a burgeoning and immediate revolution in the comics industry, McCloud outlined several key areas in which digital delivery might improve the position of artists within the larger industry. But while

Girlpants and Gasoline

McCloud envisioned digital delivery systems only as a method by which future artists might cheaply distribute their work to a theoretically infinite reader base–thereby reducing the percentage of sales profits eaten up by printing and shipping costs–since the year 2000 digital-only *webcomics* have achieved far wider success in marketing and creative strategies than the major publishing houses. Overcoming in short order many of the technological limitations McCloud saw as blocking the evolution of digital comics, the last decade has proven webcomics to have more financial and creative profits than McCloud originally conceived. Most prominently, they facilitate open dialogue between reader and artist, thereby closing–ever increasingly–the once widening gap McCloud saw between the two as a result of growing complexity in print media.

Analysis and Discussion of McCloud's Chief Arguments

Throughout McCloud's three graphic dissertations (Understanding Comics, Reinventing Comics and Making Comics) and continuing lecture circuit, his greatest point of contention with the comics industry lay in increasing complexity of production. While this allots for a wider audience, it abstracts the artist and the readers from each other, a loss of communication for which the creative work ultimately suffers. McCloud believed an attempt to reproduce a work for a broader audience necessitated in the artist "compromise in two ways: First, a piece of [the profits] pay for the copies. Second, the copies may vary from the original in appearance and quality." This additional step between creation and sale of a work adds a level of complexity that may further alter the work. An artist may, for example, alter the work in such a way as to better accommodate not its legibility, but its reproduction. These were McCloud's "Four Effects" of mass-production on an artwork: increased complexity, modification of the original, siphoned profits, and creative alteration.

As readership increases, an artist will find more and more of her time being taken up by the task of printing and delivering her art. As McCloud put it, "Enter the publisher. Now the artist can go back to work and let someone else do the selling. The publisher uses a professional printer (and pre-print house) and a simple distribution method." Here again the Four Effects come into play: as extra steps are added between artist and reader, further alteration of the original occurs from paper to printer to pulp. Fewer profits, then, go directly to the artist and the work's continued existence becomes reliant on the publisher's approval of its content.

This last bit is perhaps most dangerous, as the initial sale of a comic is based on a reader seeing something he likes and deciding to compensate the creator monetarily. As complexity of production increases, more concern is placed on the continued production of the product and the creative paths necessary to ensure this. Less concern, therefor, is had for the reader's original taste, which began the whole process.

Digital delivery, McCloud hypothesized, was a theoretically open-ended solution to problematic distribution philosophies. A comic appearing online has no physical shape and can thus be downloaded by a reader, interring very low shipping and distribution costs[1]. McCloud openly favored a system by which artists made their works available online for a very low fee (compared to print comics) which would "create a readership with ten times the buying power," essentially making up low per-unit prices with greater sales quantities and wider variety for the reader's dollar.

McCloud argued that there were, in 2000, only four benefits that print media maintained over the idea of online comics, but also three major technological issues to be overcome before digital comics could start becoming profitable. Of the four benefits of print media, McCloud recognized the established industry had built-in

Girlpants and Gasoline

infrastructures for

a. cheap reproduction of titles,
b. cheap distribution of products,
c. advertising for and by outside sources–as well as self-promotion–all of which
d. relieved the artist of much responsibility, allowing him to concentrate on producing more artwork of a higher artistic quality.

As for the technological hurdles, McCloud saw The Print Industry's lower per-unit production costs and wider distribution both easily overcome by a **revolutionary form of digital downloading** some time in the near future. Existing only as easily duplicated bits of data with very low storage fees, online comics could be created and uploaded once, but downloaded any number of times by any person from effectively anywhere, thus reducing both per-unit production and distribution costs to nearly zero. More problematic were issues of **advertisement** and **time costs**. Print publishers had a heavy advantage over digital delivery systems in that they could promote their own titles through ad space in any of their own publications, ensuring visibility for a particular new title amongst similar, well-established titles. Online, McCloud believed, access to a comic would be physically controlled by a reader's Internet Service Provider (ISP) and the reader's foreknowledge of the comic's web address. Worse, it forced the artist to spend less time, effort and money on the actual *production* of a comic and more on getting it online and *noticed*.

On top of these problems, McCloud noted technological roadblocks like then-current availability and costs of computers, clarity of digital images on contemporary monitors and rather lengthy load-times for images and data-intensive work online. However these issues, McCloud admitted, were much more quickly being improved upon as technology rapidly progressed, though as ten years ago most computer screens were still well below the the resolution threshold necessary to compete with the printed words and images, and those models which were were not exactly what an average consumer would call "affordable." Load time, meanwhile, was still restricted to the refresh rate of 28 and 56K dial-up modems, a serious concern when the alternative was flipping a printed page. These issues too, McCloud argued, would be overcome and in much shorter order, but until then digital delivery of comics would not be a viable, profitable option for graphic artists.

More Recent History: The Technological Advent of Webcomics

Much as McCloud predicted, technology has made great leaps forward since the release of *Reinventing Comics*. The costs of high-end computers drops quarterly while base-model technology steadily improves.[2] All new computers are now HD media compatible, while some have moved beyond utilizing an optical drive at all. Even the most basic PCs feature screen resolutions more than capable of viewing comic pages in a reasonable clarity. Several brands of software exist for this very purpose. Jomic and CDisplay are popular third-party 'comic book reader' applications, functioning as the comic book equivalent of e-book readers across operating systems. Utilizing the .CBR Comic Book Archive file format, these programs allow users to view full pages of scanned comics or other sequential image groups in a variety of formats at high resolution.

Second generation e-readers, such as Amazon's Kindle or the Barnes & Noble Nook, allow for the same mobility of reading material as keeping a rolled-up comic book in one's backpack. While these are essentially text-only devices, the appeal has spurred application development of full-picture comic book readers for the newest generation of smart phones and tablet computers, chiefly the Apple iPhone/iPod Touch/iPad and smartphones utilizing Android operating systems. These applications, however, have more problems than their copyright gray-area desktop brethren. (More on that later.)

Online, finally, the "Web 2.0" movement resulted in the emergence of new websites hosting higher-bandwidth content and running under the base assumption that nearly all users already possessed high-speed internet connections through either home or local establishments.

With technological impediments overcome, the only lead print publishing still seems to have over digitized comicing is the Publishing Industry's ability to take on the workload of distribution and advertising that would otherwise fall to the artist. This need, however, has given rise to various web sites and services which provide many of these benefits *exclusively* to web-based cartoonists. Comic Genesis (formerly "Keenspace"), for example provides free server hosting to thousands of separate webcomics in return for the placement of one Keenspace ad and one external banner ad somewhere on the comic's main page. Not only does this completely eradicate the hosting cost for webspace, it answers in part McCloud's question of how to find new comics online; if a reader were to visit one comic hosted on the C.G. network, she would also view at least one ad for *another* comic hosted by the same company, the same way an advertisement for The Hulk might be found in a Thor comic. If this reader were to only view a few strips of that one comic, she would encounter a new ad for a new comic on each page, thus broadening the readership associated with all of those comics while remaining relatively unobtrusive to the flow of reading.

Profitability

With the logistical shortcomings of producing independent webcomics vanishing, how can webcomics become *profitable?* In a few cases, Scott McCloud's prediction of free-or-cheap downloads for full issues or trade volumes of comics was a hole-in-one. Certain services like WOWIO offer written fiction and comic downloads either very cheaply or for free outright, relying on quantity of small purchases and outside advertising to compensate for the small cost of digitally hosting and distributing their content.

Dave Willis (creator of *Roomies!* and its sequels/spin-offs *It's Walky!*, *Joyce and Walky!*, *Shortpacked!*, *and Dumbing of Age*), as well as other artists like *Penny and Aggie*'s creative team of T. Campbell and Gisèle Lagacé employ a similar "Free vs. Premium" content business model. Their current projects update on their regular schedules for free, but readers willing to make a monthly donation to *Joyce and Walky!* or *Penny & Aggie* are treated to additional comics and extras like exclusive desktop artwork. Josh Lesnick, notably of webcomics *Wendy* and *Girly*, meanwhile, makes a living primarily by hosting Slipshine, a subscription-only service hosting and publishing dozens of "adult" oriented webcomics.[3]

Still, webcomics have been accepted as a free part of the internet. The same as legally downloading music or movies, if a product is available for free (or can be as easily duped as a simple image), then few people are going to be willing to pay for that same product. Since this is the case, webcomics must rely on other business models for their chief source of income. Usually, it's The Store.

Randy K. Milholland, debauched mind behind the long-running webcomic *Something*Positive*, once (I hope) laughingly tweeted, "Another thread of 'LOL *webcartoonists*, more like *t-shirt vendors* AMIRITE?!' on *DailyCartoonist [dot] com*. Jesus Christ." Like most webcartoonists, Milholland–who has drawn *S*P* regularly since 2001–works in addition to cartooning, often appearing on stage in Boston's theatre community. The profits from *Something Positive* come from banner advertisements and reader donations, but most prolifically the *S*P* Store, in which Milholland sells original artwork, prints and of course hilarious apparel, and ever so occasionally print

Girlpants and Gasoline

editions of his side comic *Supor Stupor*.

Though Milholland jokes, much of the profitability of web-comics stems from merchandise sales, the same way Jim Davis licensed the *Garfield* image to everything from greeting cards to books and plush car window clings. If a web artist has a large enough or loyal enough readership, she may offer a shirt design for presale by one of several means. If she gets enough pre-orders, she may be able to afford a limited run of clothing. If demand stays high, she can continue to order more shirts from her printing company and sell them on a regular basis. Unlike the publishing industry's business model of selling the product as well as associated toys and merchandise, webcomics and their artists tend to subsist on the sale of their ad space and merchandise, while the original product continues to be offered up for free. This method of course relies heavily on the loyalty and sense of community within a readership.

A comic's online store might be as simple as an Etsy account or a template PayPal store, where orders are placed and shipped directly by the artist (or spouses, or unpaid intern slaves). Specialty stores have also risen to provide resources for artists wishing to sell merchandise collectively. Operating out of rented studio space MegaGear.com is the exclusive online store for merchandise from Fred Gallagher's smash-hit, long-form Original English Language Manga *MegaTokyo*. Run by Gallagher's wife, Sarah, MegaGear was originally a small, in-home operation. Over years, the shop expanded to incorporate other artists' work, notably that of *AppleGeeks* artist Mohammad F. Haque. On a grander scale, Jeffrey Rowland, in addition to his two webcomics *Wigu* and *Overcompensating*, runs TopatoCo, online store for nearly four dozen other comics. This collaboration extends to group functions at comic conventions, sales, cross-promotion and occasional crossover shenanigans.

In May of 2010, CNN ran an online article for its tech blog by Larry Frum, entirely focussed on the existential merits of wearing webcomic t-shirts. *CNN*. Frum's opening line is, "As the old saying goes, 'clothing makes the man.' In the geek culture, what is said **on** the clothing is more important than the clothing itself." Shane Peterman of ThinkGeek.com then adds, "Your shirt helps you identify who is 'in the know.'" It's another iteration of striated levels of coolness within a clique. However, Peterman points out the recurring trend of newer post-postmodernist thinking. It's not about having a *cooler* shirt, it's about the subtle expression of possessing the *knowledge* of having a cooler shirt. Look awesome, be awesomer. Rub it in everyone's face by not rubbing it in everyone's face and be awesomest. Dave Malki ![4], artist behind woodcut-stylized webcomic Wondermark and "Supreme Commander of Publicity & Promotions for TopatoCo" according to his bio page, sums it up so succinctly it's like he crawled into my closet and slithered out wearing my "Irony" t-shirt: "The shirt shows the exclusivity and uniqueness of the wearer. …It makes them seem super cool."

Very, very rarely, a webcomic will become super-profitable.[5] *MegaTokyo* and *Apple Geeks*, along with *Penny Arcade* are some of the more well-known examples, so popular and long-running that their influence has spread well beyond digital publishing. All three have in the past several years enjoyed print editions published by mainstream comic publisher Dark Horse Media[6]. In these instances, rather than working for a publishing company on another artist's creation or altering one's original work to befit the creative whims of that specific publisher, artists and their works have been *sought out* by a leading comic publisher. Though many webcomic artists participate in small print runs for their readers, more and more successful webcomics are being sold in major bookstores, offering proof that a free digital comic can be made independently profitable enough for larger publishers to take note. Webcomic artists *can* make a profit while retaining complete creative integrity of their works. Moreover, print publishers are beginning to accept the idea of taking a creative backseat to the needs of both artists and readers.

Girlpants and Gasoline

Reconnection: Communication and Community Between Reader and Artist

More even than in print, the success of a webcomic is dependent on its readership for survival. A book can linger in pre-publishing for decades. A poorly-received sequel still has to be *purchased*. Webcomic artists *must* communicate with their fan base to keep it, and–to some extent–appease it constantly and for *free*. While print publishing abstracts the artist from the reader, the internet allows and even requires modes of communication between the two parties, to a far greater degree that anything seen at large publishing companies.

At the most basic level, nearly every webcomic contains (somewhere) a link to email the artist. This provides at least some method by which a reader can address her concerns to the comic's creator. More often, webcomics also feature a News Box in which the comic's creator can provide relevant information, for example: links to related sites and comics, new merchandise in the store, relevant news stories or their attendance and whereabouts during upcoming comic conventions. These modes of communication can certainly be more direct than, say, writing fanmail to a print artist, but are still by nature unidirectional.

Twitter has become something of a more immediate method of two-way communication between readers and artists. Due chiefly to the network's prominence–especially so after traditional news media became aware of its existence–both artist and reader probably already have Twitter accounts. A reader needs only to click a button to begin receiving 140-character updates from their favorite artists regarding everything from whether the next comic update is going to be a little late to what was for dinner or even (in many, most probably facetious cases) exactly how drunk an artist has to be while creating their life's work. Yet in the other direction, depending on how often artists check their "@" replies, artists can hold entire conversations with fans and other creators in an open, public forum. While print comics usually feature "Letters to the Editor" segments in their afterwords, there is very little direct back-and-forth communication between reader and artist. At best, a few letters will be printed in part, usually because they A) praise the work and B) ask a question that was repeatedly raised since last month's issue. With Twitter, however, both users find themselves equals. Entire conversations can be held instantly, while a landslide of questions or comments in a specific vein is felt directly by the artist, instead of, say, an underpaid mail-room clerk tasked with summarization of monthly letter trends.

Discussing the failings of current publishing standards over his own Twitter account, Randy Milholland tweets, "If the comics syndicates die, will anyone miss them besides syndicated cartoonists? Oh no! No more Christian cavemen! This is a loss?" Almost in sync, Josh Lesnick tweets simply, "I feel nothing for newspaper comics." But like any group, all webcomic artists are not of the same mind. Danielle Corsetto of Girls With Slingshots utilizes her Twitter account more for the brief updates on her life that the site was designed for, though she also utilizes it to better suit her comic to her readers. Corsetto has inquired as to the best way to write "Kiss the Cook" in 'bad German,' check realistic British idioms, solicited names for secret agents, even going so far as to solicit reader requests for bonus material on the site and in her GWS print volumes. When her print volumes hit their third pressing, she offered a special discount and free custom sketches to Twitter followers who purchased copies. Corsetto has a dedicated readership, to which she appears just as dedicated.

Probably the oldest open center for webcomic discussion, though, is the forum, in which users register to complain a lot and get into off-topic discussions that once related to a particular comic. Artists and writers, and occasionally their friends and relatives moderated the boards and sometimes jumped in to give hints, encouragement or perhaps an off-color comment about one user's mother.

Girlpants and Gasoline

While a few larger comics continue to host their own forums, many have switched over to any of the currently popular blogging services that allow artists their own space for their thoughts, as well as imbedded comment threads on their comic's original webpage. And of course, dated and titled blog entries are much easier to sift through than a page of most-recently-updated threads.

Ryan North of Dinosaur Comics posts to his long-form blog, "The death of newspapers is going to be great for comics, you guys! ...Most comics appearing in newspapers are BLAND. Terribly, similarly, depressingly bland." It's the same argument McCloud made in Reinventing Comics for the downturn in print comic publishing during the nineteen-eighties: there is little or no reader-artist interaction in print comics, be it newspaper syndication or a major monthly publishing house. Milholland's views, North's and Lesnick's all come from individuals with tight-knit communities of fans who are willing and able to voice their opinions directly to the artists.

Milholland still maintains a separate message board for Something Positive, which features discussion threads for each week of comics, favorite characters, recent or related news and even fan art (including fiction and music). Besides sifting through his copious quantities of irate hate-mail[7], Milholland takes an active role on his message boards, joining the discussion as an equal participant who keeps a somewhat open mind while retaining final say in his finished product. Conversing freely with his fans, Milholland learns how they feel about specific aspects of his work and this allows him to continually re-craft his comic in such ways as to make it more successful while maintaining a creative path he feels comfortably suits the work. He has expanded plots around tangential characters, giving them much larger roles than he originally intended, both because the characters become well-liked and because it improves the over-all story.[8]

Milholland also enjoys taking reader expectations and destroying them in the most fun ways possible, again to better the plot, though sometimes simply to stir up trouble amongst his fan base and weed out the less supportive readers.[9] Though not necessarily a wise decision for an artist looking to broaden his readership, this move does ensure quality over quantity in both Milholland's comic and its community; long-time readers stay and respect his artistic control, as well as the notion that Something Positive can at times be comic, tragic or serious with as little warning before one as the other.

It is the community surrounding a webcomic that makes it profitable, both financially and creatively. As McCloud says, "Most people will never pay for web content." While some artists continue to place donation boxes on their main pages, a webcomic's livelihood is its store and its loyal readership, and the former cannot precede the latter. The two-way communication offered by artists through their blogs, forums and Twitter accounts fosters a sense of community and the growth of a successful, eventually profitable artistic product in a medium unhindered by the distance or logistical complexity that impedes creativity and innovation in print publishing.

Digital Toxicity: Are Webcomics Killing Print?

Put simply, no. It's thermodynamically impossible to hold a conversation about the webcomics industry without mentioning Scott Kurtz[10]. Kurtz is the artist behind *PvP* ("Player vs. Player"), one of the longest-running webcomics, launched in 1998. He has also become one of the internet's leading proponents of digital comics. In a great interview he did for The Washington Post's "Comic Riffs" blog to promote his Macworld panel at the beginning of the year, Kurtz defended his bread and butter as not the cause or even result of Print Media's death, likening it more to the parallel existence and evolution of Cro-Magnons and Neanderthal Man than to dinosaurs and a hurtling comet:

Girlpants and Gasoline

> Anyone who tells you that the internet is killing newspapers is full
> of it. Newspapers don't have to die in order for [internet comics] to
> succeed. Same goes for the opposite. My largest source of reliable
> income is selling print collections of my book. My most reliable
> revenue streams are based in the same traditional models that
> syndicated cartoonists have been employing for years. Newspapers
> are dying concurrent to us, not because of us.

Print Comics Publishers really have three choices in how they
deal with the advent of digital comics. Either they can bury their
heads in the sand and pretend webcomics aren't real, embrace the
freedom of artistry and cost digital comics bring forth, or they can
fight tooth and nail against the idea every step of the way, trying in
vain to curtail illicit operations which fight against them. And not
surprisingly, they manage to employ all three options simultaneously.

But first, some background: When major Print Publishers hear
"digital comics" they tend to wet themselves, not because they fear
the weekly, four-panel adventures of anthropomorphic house pets but
because they're thinking of *comic scans*. Scans are to DC and Marvel
what the MP3 is to Music Executives. Every week faithful, diligent
men and women engage in a digital war of copyright infringement
and comic piracy. Yes, they scan hundreds of new comics, clean up
the images, bundle them into the tight .CBR format that legitimate
artists use to share their own works and upload the packs to various
websites and torrent-based downloading networks. It's the same
problem the RIAA has faced every day since Napster went live back
in 1999: A product is offered both at a price and for free. Which will
the average consumer choose? Obviously free.

And that's not an unreasonable choice! How can one properly
test whether or not one *enjoys* an artistic work without experiencing
it to some degree? There have been plenty of songs I couldn't stand at
first, but I caught looping endlessly in the back of my head days later.
Download a song, play it a few dozen times and you're free. No need
to buy the whole album. Eventually the RIAA discovered it was best

139

to work *with* the internet rather than against it. Legal downloading sites gained support as prices dropped to what consumers thought to be more reasonable levels, and the RIAA cut back on prosecuting grandmothers for illegal downloading when they realized it was terribly cost-ineffective and made them come off looking like greedy assholes.

Marvel hasn't been in the news for prosecuting kids downloading the latest issues of *X-Men*, but they're feeling the sting. Before digital comics, if you wanted to see whether or not you'd be interested in buying a comic book, you'd have to go down to the comic shop and flip pages until the clerk loudly informed you that you were *not* in a library, then either bring the comic up to the counter or set the thing back on its shelf. However, in most towns you're now less likely to find an open comic shop than the latest DCP-Scans on BitTorrent.

The problem for Large Comics Publishers is not having a network analogous to radio; there's no free-to-air distribution system where consumers can get a taste for the hottest, newest comics. Well, I shouldn't really say that. On their websites, Large Comics Publishers frequently post *previews* of newly-released issues, more akin to a digital music store's song preview than radio play, in that only the first few pages of the issue are available.[11] Still, like the music industry discovered, once the whole is available for free, who really remains willing to buy a physical copy?

Well, truthfully, a lot of people. Reading hardcopy comics is benefitted by a decidedly more tactile experience than listening to music. Flipping pages, feeling the paper in one's hand, even the smell of fresh or age-worn trade pages is part of an experience digital comics can't offer up. Anyone who has laid awake at night salivating over The Food Network knows how it feels to be a die-hard Print Comics fan trying to read a scan.

And scans are not without their own flaws. Chiefly, I'm sure any attorney reading this would point out that they are *by nature*

Girlpants and Gasoline

illegal. They are as much copyright infringement as that copy of ZoSo your friend burned for you in college. More pertinently (to the savvy internet pirates out there), the availability of specific scans is entirely dependent on popularity. Every week's issue of *Batman* will arrive like clockwork, but the pirates who spend their hours canning and seeding print comics aren't going to waste their time with series no one asks to read. Warren Ellis, award-winning writer, having worked titles both large and small for DC and Marvel, in addition to independent works, posted this to his "Whitechapel" message board/ blog back in April of 2010:

> Aside from the odd fluke, pirated comics tend to be exactly what you'd expect....It is, in fact, generally the same skew you'd get in a standard comics shop. All the new Marvels, all the new DCs, most of Vertigo and a smattering of the other stuff. If I were starting out today, I'd be thinking very hard about wrapping my comic into a .cbz container, slinging it on Rapidshare and posting the link on download sites under an anonymous handle.

Whitechapel, it should be noted, is the message board for one of Ellis' ongoing projects, *Freakangels*, a title published online weekly, six pages at a time and *for free*. The comic is progressively collected into trade volumes that are sold alongside apparel and other *Freakangels* merchandise through Avatar Press. If I may use his own dialogue to establish Ellis' credibility in discussing free and paid comics in both digital and printed mediums, "Trust the fuckhead."

Rather than try and fight the losing battle against digitization, major publishers Marvel and DC have chosen to foster the iTunes business model of web distribution, supporting third-party digital comic shops with their own reader platforms, designed to work with the publishers' proprietary file types.

In 2010 I had the pleasure of attending New York Comic Con as a member of the press, freelancing for a local podcast. My attention had been caught by a Professionals panel on the events schedule titled "Digital Comics and Distribution." Since I was forced to miss Scott Kurtz's webcomics panel that weekend, I was excited to see another panel focus so intently on this particular aspect of internet comic media. Instead of any of the artists or topics I expected, though, I found only the sad, delusional and impotent rationalizations of bloated, aging corporations.[12]

The panel featured Ira Rubenstein, Executive V.P. of Marvel Comics' Global Digital Media group, DC Co-Publisher Jim Lee[13] and CEOs David Steignberger and Micah Baldwin of digital comic reader platforms Comixology and Graphic.ly, respectively. The panel was moderated by Buddy Scalera, a photographer and marketer who makes a (rather successful) living shooting anatomical reference material for comic book artists, posing obscenely fit men and women heroically, in their underwear.[14]

It was kind of a sad dance, watching two captains of the comics industry trying to sound like they weren't begging readers to buy their overpriced products. Around this mournful waltz, the third-party CEOs were prancing merrily, because they know that if the Big Guys want to make any money with their pay-to-read business model, they're going to have to go through third-party software, middlemen making money off an intangible product.

I quickly realized the panel has nothing to do at all with innovation within the industry, and everything to do with an all-out defensive war against comics piracy. Scans are subtly dismissed as evil and detrimental to artists, and while this is certainly *somewhat* true, every argument made against them is *for* keeping DC and Marvel in business, not the artists. To this end, some fairly spurious logic is used to downplay how awesome it is that a reader can instantly download millions of comic books free over the internet. Baldwin cites no source when he states that if only about one third of music sales are digital, then the percentage of digital comic sales must be about the same.

Girlpants and Gasoline

Rubenstein posits that agreeing on a standard file type for the comics industry will unify the technology. Obviously, he means something other than the .cbr formats, because those aren't suited for smaller mobile devices and pinching to zoom and scroll through a series of large image files becomes annoying.[15] He adds that the music industry's failure with DRM[16]-protection proved that all coding methods are ultimately hackable, so the best business model is to take the offensive. It is the publisher's responsibility, he says, to create good, digitally available comics that will crush illegal scans through higher *quality*. Lee chimes in, "Everyone has the same internet access," later adding, "All these comics are available for free on Bit Torrent. It comes down to what kind of resolution are you getting?" Rubenstein argues to make the best consumer experience possible so customers won't care about paying a little extra. Then he plugs the forthcoming Marvel Unlimited Store, offering 8-9,000 titles for a monthly fee of $9.99. PC only, at first, though the iPad app will work with Comixology. Real slick.

Steinberger, hearing his baby making endorsement money, spiels the complexity of different file formats for different devices, adds that basic encryption on a good product is all one needs, and notes that since his company also publishes independent artists' works, digital distribution could be seen as a sort of farming league for bigger publishers.

The next twenty minutes are spent with Lee, Baldwin and Steinberger promising a room full of hopeful comic artists that the more promising road to fame and fortune isn't incorporating privately and working hard or joining a publisher on another project and working up the ranks, but in giving a portion of their profits to digital delivery companies so they can reach a wider audience with less time spent on self-promotion. Somewhere, Scott McCloud was rolling over in his grave.[17] Lee makes the valid point that not everyone can be a Scott Kurtz. *PvP* is big, he admits, but "I'll just put it online and make it rich," isn't realistic. He wants to give creators a bit more room to play with while unifying digi-comics with a user's regular downloads. He argues a change in format from the 22-page vertical layout that's an industry standard. "I'm not a fan of blowing and chopping things up," he says. "It doesn't have to be 22 pages to be a good story. It could be 20 pages, or 8 pages." Stories in shorter chunks like serials, using fewer panels per page would make zooming unnecessary and solve the issue of mobile reading.[18]

Baldwin seems to take a more modest stance. "'I have an idea, can you do it?'" is how he says his company interacts with artists. Limiting a work to its intended device(s) lets more interesting uses of media come into play: looking through keyholes, clickable t-shirts and advertisement with in-comic coupons are just some of the ideas he thinks can be a whole new source of revenue. "We are just a tool," he says.

The conversation turns to motion comics, the big-budget offspring of comic books and traditional moving animation, and it's generally agreed that motion comics are undeniably too expensive for independent companies and a financial vacuum for leading publishers. Finally, Rubenstein says what everyone else on the panel has been pussyfooting around: "Digital comics is profitable, doing well, but that's *with print*." He says that it's Marvel's policy that digital sales should drive physical sales. Digital comics should be made into paper editions. Books should always come before digital. He touts the idea of releasing free issues/apps in time with physical releases. If Issue #1 goes on sale for free the week Issue #2 is released, it will drive sales of the print series.

Sadly for Ira, the argument that scans are of low quality is pretty much bunk. Webcomics and other primarily-digital artistic serial works are finding average web resolution to be more than adequate for getting exposure, while scans both legal and otherwise are finding steady use as much as illegal music sharing. I found out later that Scott Kurtz had made a very interesting point at the Comic Con panel I wasn't able to attend.

Girlpants and Gasoline

Ultimately what's going to happen is whatever the kids want to do. You talk to audiophiles and they hate MP3s, but there's study after study saying that *kids don't give a shit.*...You and I look at a painting and we can tell the difference between that and digital. But if you talk to kids and they don't give a shit and they're selling a lot of digital paintings, that's where it's going.

With this in mind, Rubenstein's last words sound less daring and all the more frightened: "Let the consumers decide."

---

[1] The cost of–*snicker*–a "dial-up" connection.

[2] In 2000 I owned three DVDs and bought a boombox. With a *cassette deck.*

[3] Lesnick actually contrasts McCloud's low opinion on the diminutive misnomers *comic strips* and *adult comics*, writing, "Calling webcomics *digital comics* is like calling all comic books *graphic novels.* In other words, it's stupid and pretentious. But at least it makes it sound kinda futuristic. Like digital watches. Digital watches are pretty futuristic."

[4] The exclamation point is a mandatory, albeit self-appointed honorific and suffix.

[5] By *internet* standards. Essentially, "just-profitable-enough-to-count-as-a-real-job," plus maybe a little extra.

[6] Issues 4-6 of *MegaTokyo* were picked up by one of the "Big Two," DC Comics, 4 and 5 under the now defunct CMX imprint.

[7] Milholland is openly atheistic, joking that he received more angry e-mails for having his protagonist casually mention that he believes what a person does in life is important (more so, as he doesn't believe in an afterlife) than when Milholland spent a week showcasing corrupt, Jesus-touting politicians and satirized Ann Coulter, claiming she eats babies.
Incidentally, Milholland is also a big fan of blocking Twitter users who complain too much but never seem to simply stop following his account

[8] Pepito, originally a Latino midget sex slave won in a poker game, was freed and went on to become a greedy millionaire who was later eaten alive by a ravenous band of preteen schoolgirls in cat ears, much to the delight of fans everywhere.

[9] Trying to limit the extent to which *S*P* was autobiographical, Milholland killed off the character based on his own (still living) mother and gave his (healthy) "father" Alzheimer's, forever scaring readers into thinking that at any moment any one of their most beloved cast members could die horribly. Of course this is much more true to life, and so may bruise their tender, succulent, juicy psyches.

[10] I think he comes to your home and stomps on your pets until you mention him. I've heard ... *things.*

[11] Of course they are still ad-supported and occasionally censored in part, and you can't

ever find the really fun, *interesting* stuff you're actually into, so in those regards I guess comic previews are *a lot* like the radio.

[12] Not judgmental at all.

[13] Lee rose to prominence as an artist for Marvel before leaving to help found independent publisher Image Comics, then took the big chair at DC. He gets around.

[14] If you've ever wondered why so many action shots tend to look the same in mainstream superhero comics, it's because the artists all use Buddy's books and CD-Rom anatomy guides. This ensures there is only *one* man creepily asking to photograph half-naked people instead of an army of model-poor comic artists. Truly, his is a noble sacrifice.

[15] Which *is* the case. Plus, those are open-source and he can't make money off that.

[16] "Digital Rights Management"

[17] At the time of this writing, Mr. McCloud is only 53 years old and very much alive. I in no way meant to imply ill will towards him, only that the arguments presented above were so painfully backward that I assume he must have gone out behind his home, dug a large pit in the backyard, hopped inside and tried rolling around in it for a bit just to see how it felt.

[18] I picture McCloud now inviting the family dog down into his hole with him.

ZOMBIES: THE HUNGRY NIHILISTS

I seriously need to stop *trying* to dream about zombies. Last night was nothing but running through an infected dorm and by the time I got to a safe attic, it was just some fat guy and two toddlers, one of whom was infected and bit me so I had to wash my arm off with mint mouthwash. And I *hate* mint."

"Zombies are just hungry nihilists." Aside from being an epic name for the screamo masterpiece my prog-rock band is going to release after our album entirely about *SNL* "Celebrity Jeopardy!" jokes, this is actually a huge revelation for me. Nihilists believe in the futility of existence, if you can even call that a belief since I'm also somehow sure they refuse to believe in anything. But what could a nihilist *value*? Ostensibly, knowledge, the one useful tool with which to advance oneself in life until he dies, staving off that final black end as long as possible in an admittedly doomed effort. It's also the one thing a man can truly hold as his own without fear of theft by anything short of that same abyssal death.

David E. Zucker

And what do zombies say, if they say anything at all? "Brains...." Of course most modern zombies don't actually say much of anything, and they're pretty indiscriminate in what parts of you they will eat. Surprisingly, they seem to be fond of entrails, right-side necks and left arms, in particular. I'm not sure why the left. Probably has something to do with the heart being on the left and Americans' high-cholesterol diet. However beyond this, there isn't some great existential need for zombies seeking brains. They are the ultimate nihilists: empty shells of creatures, devoid of souls or humanity, truly everything but their basest animal instincts, unnatural, cannibal monstrosities feeding with all the intelligence and purpose of locusts, refusing death itself but in doing so robbed of any value or meaning. They persist whilst we fight amongst ourselves, slowly adding to their number. They are obscenely other, patient, unrelenting, and unavoidable.

And they're still fucking hungry. That might punch a little hole in the dark hearts of nihilists out there but, hey, I make enemies like Apple's Chinese Foxconn workers make intricate LCD screens by the dozen. And by that I mean they kill themselves. And become zombies. Conveniently, there are no OSHA-comparable standards for the undead. Or the Chinese, I guess.

THE TRUTH ABOUT CATS AND DOGS

I am going to be very honest with you. I have never seen Cyrano de Bergerac, nor do I even like the Police song "Roxanne." Neither have I seen *The Truth About Cats & Dogs* and actually rather dislike Uma Thurman's face, though like all good misanthropes I harbor an unrequited geek-crush on Janeane Garofalo. I am willing to bet this is for the same reasons I still prefer cats over dogs.

I know, I'm a traitor to men everywhere, men whose ancestors hunted with their semi-tamed wolf partners to bring down enormous prey and eat its delicious, delicious flesh-bits. Well, fuck that. Dogs smell bad. I know men smell bad, but I personally try really hard not to smell *too* bad. I'm not even allergic to dander in the slightest, I just don't like how dogs smell. I don't like that the scent gets all over you immediately after you touch one, that it's not even completely water soluble and takes some serious scrubbing to get off. Cats? Cats are fucking OCD about bathing themselves. On top of that they don't actually *do* much all day. They don't get tired and then pant because they can't sweat. When a cat gets overheated running around the house with no discernible agenda besides knocking into things and toppling your Hummel figures, it just knows to cut it the hell out and lay down for a while. Which raises a big plus for me:

Cats are lazy. Not only does this keep them from smelling just awful–or at all; you really have to get a faceful of cat to smell much of anything–it also means they don't require a lot of maintenance. Feed a cat and change its litter box every so often. The cat will take care of the rest himself. That's because a cat doesn't give a crap about you. If its master dies, a dog will starve to death waiting by its human's side. A cat would eat your eyelids before you were fucking cold. It'd still have food left *in the kitchen*.

Cats are dicks. We recognize our own. They appreciate my bluntness, my honesty and my aloof attitude. The nastiest cats in the world love me, because I don't cause them grief and I don't pump out fear-mones like they're paleolithic giants and I'm a tiny, wounded gazelle of some kind (an impala, perhaps). A cat's opinion of you is primarily based on how little you piss them off, which, incidentally, also explains my taste in women.

Do you know what it feels like to get that unconditional love from a pet or another human being? Doesn't it feel much better when you actually *respect* the other creature as its own entity? When you feel like you've earned that love and deserve it?

Of course it doesn't. You're dog people. All you want is some-one to throw you another stick and roll over.

ON INTERNET PREORDERS

I'm told credit cards are a display of trust, in me, on the part of the credit companies. They *trust* that I'll be able to pay them back for fronting me some cash. They also trust that if I'm even a little late, they can fine and surcharge the hell out of me, up to the point where I have to declare bankruptcy and can never again get a credit card with anything resembling a decent interest rate. That's called getting "black-balled," kids and kidettes.

It's a lot like loan-sharking; or I more accurately suspect, loan-sharking is a lot like credit companies, insofar as it's closer to the original, dirty, pound-of-flesh industry/sin of simony. I think the only difference is that loan sharks retain that right to physically assault you if you default, instead of just ruining you with an endless financial miasma. Suffice it to say a loan shark will help you pay off a legitimate hospital bill and a credit card might pay off the hospital bill for not paying your loan shark, but neither will loan you money to pay the bill they personally send you[1].

Even money says if there is anything in this universe that

151

David E. Zucker

karmically balances credit card companies, it's internet pre-orders. I pay a company some money up-front, and *I* trust *them* to deliver the product when they say they will. "Duke Nukem Forever" notwithstanding, this generally tends to hold up. I even get a *discount* for giving them money before they deserve it, for giving away my money for *nothing*. And all the while the instant-gratification-Netflix-torrenting-YouTube lobes of my brain are telling me I got to charge *them* for *unreasonably* withholding from me something that is *currently unavailable*[2].

The few times things just die, you generally get your money back, so everyone's on board with this system. Preorders get products advance capital, and corporations an active gauge of consumer interest. Hell, the website KickStarter has risen to prominence with the sole purpose of taking donations and pre-orders for projects and then *only* charge buyers' accounts if a set minimum for funding is reached within an allotted timespan. It's crowd-sourced, home-brewed pre-order.

But here's the magic: as much as you dread getting your credit card bill come January, bits of tinsel and wrapping paper still cloistered in the far corners of your living room, the potato-y taste of latkes still on your breath weeks later, internet pre-orders are a wonderful, opposite experience. I pre-ordered the complete *Star Wars* Saga blu-ray collection a *year* before it came out. With the discount, I paid something like 38% of the retail price. It was glorious. More glorious because back when I bought it I had *money*. I could *afford* to spend $80 on a 9-disc collection of six movies I've already bought thrice-over. Could I have afforded it when it finally went on sale? Not so much. But back when I ordered I was rolling in it. For something I was inevitably buying, it was a fantastic opportunity.

Then I forgot about it.

I honestly forgot about it every few months, until a geekery news site made brief mention of it and for one split second I would worry about affording it, until I remembered I'd already handled the

Girlpants and Gasoline

situation. It felt like that spooky-but-awesome feeling of saving the day through time travel magic at the end of a *Bill and Ted* movie. Somehow, I *knew* this would happen and I went *back in time* to save myself *before* I was poor. "Hey, it was me who stole my dad's keys!"

One day, my favorite thing in the universe simply arrived on my doorstep as if by some kind of Jedi mind trick. And I even got to improve my credit score.

---

[1] Except maybe those little checks you get in the mail offering to transfer your balances with no fee, but that's still a scam; it's just designed to have you pay *them* more and their competitors less. I got a guy named Vito who can do the same thing with no questions asked.
[2] Or they're just banking that the product will be over-produced and hit the SALE aisle within a month, forcing me to lament even the discounted price I paid for it.

PHONE BOOTHS, DeLOREANS, AND JAKE GYLLENHAAL:

Time Travel Explodes Your Brain

I have no idea why more Think Tanks and opera houses aren't built in the shape of giant shower stalls; the acoustics are perfect, there's white noise, and with the gentle splash of hard water trickling down your back, inducing minor breakouts as condensation begins to fog the air, two things happen: first, you can sing like a rock star. The second is a complete expansion of one's mind to fill every recess of the imagination, finding solutions to the greatest puzzles in mankind's history so startlingly simple and profound they are more *apriori* realization than original thought.

For example, I once came up with a method for faster-than-light (FTL) communications, but it necessitated the prior existence and use of two quantum supercomputers running a trinary programming language based on the quantum entanglement of charged particles, and then transporting one to a distant location via sublight

Girlpants and Gasoline

means. Another time I figured out what happened at the end of *Donnie Darko*[1].

I've drawn out the chronology of *Terminator* on fogged glass numerous times. And *Bill and Ted*. And *Primer*. 'I think about time travel way too often,' is probably what I'm getting at, here. I basically grew up on *Back to the Future* and, short of *Star Wars*, it was probably the only trilogy in existence to my tiny, developing brain, and that's probably why watching Doc and Marty now gives me the same uneasy feeling as watching the *Star Wars* prequels. It just doesn't work. Flux capacitors and Japanese components aside, the 'logic' of *BttF*'s time travel isn't internally consistent after the first movie, but if we're going to prove this, we're going to need a primer[2] for time travel in film.

First, some general terminology:

- "Universe" – This seems like an easy one, right? It's where everything happens. Forever. All of it is here.

- "Time" – Actually incredibly hard to explain, since only people are sentient and can notice that things seem to happen *after* their causes. For our purposes, "Time" is the general flow of events in the preferred direction of increasing entropy. People get old, plutonium decays, stars burn out and black holes swallow damned-near everything. Time goes that way.

- "Causality" – When something is done, other things happen because of it. Drop a ball and it falls to the floor. It does not generally hit the floor before you let go of it.

- "Fate/Destiny/Predestination/Predetermination" – Everything that has been, is, or will ever happen was going to

155

have happened since the crux of the Big Bang and there's nothing anyone can do to go against this. To varying degrees by interpretation, free will *is* an illusion and we're all basically meat robots playing out thermodynamic equations.

- "Timeline" - Past, present, and future laid out in nice chronological order as seen by an outside observer. Observers within a timeline will only notice a linear flow of events from their own perspective. Typically, one would look like this:

Figure 1. A basic timeline

- "Time Machine" -The means by which one "jumps" between disparate points on a timeline. Not necessarily a machine, but possibly also a wormhole or tesseract of some kind, or divine/sufficiently advanced scientific/magical influence.

With those distinctions made, it is now possible to understand the use of time travel in a narrative. More pretty diagrams have been provided for moments when you feel something behind one of your eyes starting to pop.

Causal Loops

Girlpants and Gasoline

The simplest time travel storyline involves a Causality Loop. Causal loops are created when one or more characters step back in time and, unwittingly, cause the very events that lead to them going back in time:

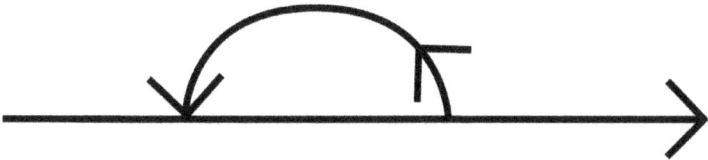

Figure 2. Causal Loop

Terminator: At some time in the near future, John Connor becomes the savior of humanity by defeating a robot army that subjugated humanity after August 29, 1997. In a last-ditch attempt to undo this, the machines send a single assassin-bot back to 1984 with the mission of assassinating all woman in a local area who share the name "Sarah Connor," presuming correctly that one of them must be John's mother. Having learned of this plan, John's forces send back their own soldier, a man named Kyle Reese, to protect Sarah. Reese is successful, though he dies in the process, but during his mission he ends up fathering John, something Sarah says she will tell as part of his lifelong training to fight the machines. Not only do the machines cause the birth of the man who beats them back, but that man is his entire life aware of and waiting to meet a younger version of his father, to task him with the semi-divine quest of going back in time to do John's mom.

This creates a paradox: the future has to happen 'before' the past can happen to cause that same future. Causality would seem to say that events in the future cannot influence the past, but the implementation of a time machine means an individual's timeline need no longer hold to the broader timeline, and that means they could theoretically affect the past. So two possibilities emerge: either all events are predetermined, as seems to be the case with Terminator, or it is possible to alter the past and change the future from that point forward.

Bill and Ted: Two kids with disinterest so severe it might be classified as a learning disability are aided in 'studying' for a history final presentation by George Carlin, an agent of wise men and women from a future of peace and prosperity, founded on the principles laid out by the eponymous Bill and Ted's rock band, Wyld Stallyns. The two bunny hop through time acquiring historical personages, learn enough to present these figures with some coherence and an inordinately well-prepared laser light show, and succeed in passing their class, their grade, and not getting sent off to military school in Alaska. Thus, the timeline is preserved, even if it's a giant squiggle of time-yarn.

Figure 3. Bill and Ted have an excellent adventure

Later, an angry old man sends robot duplicates back in time to kill Bill and Ted before they become famous. He succeeds, but the dimwitted duo best Death in multiple board games, sneak into heaven and are directed by God to two (dead?) aliens collectively named Station, which build "Good Robot Us-es" to fight the evil robots. The two are returned to life and best Angry Old Guy using gratuitously circuitous time travel off-camera, and finally learn to play their

Girlpants and Gasoline

instruments over 18 months before time traveling back to that precise moment, married and with babies named for each other, finally able to rock.[3]

Rewriting History

Back to the Future: Marty travels back in time thirty years to 1955. He accidentally prevents his parents from meeting the way he had always been told they met and, at the encouragement of Doc Brown to avoid causing a possibly universe-shattering paradox, conspires a series of elaborate and humorous ruses designed to get his parents together 'again' while fixing the time machine developed by Doc in 1985. He achieves this, and when he arrives home, he finds his life and those of his family greatly improved, as his meddling with the timestream caused his father to be a more assertive person throughout his life. Marty has overwritten his original timeline with a new history, the new 'present' supersedes the one Marty came from.

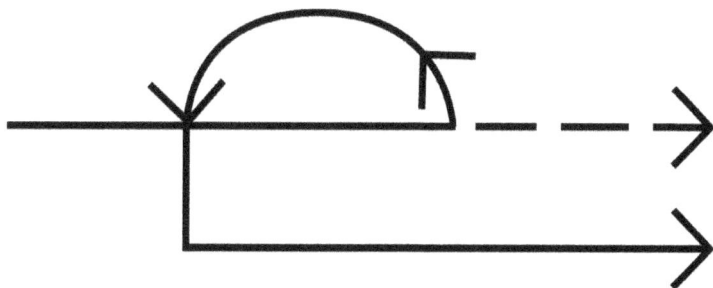

Figure 4. Rewriting a timeline

This is also the vehicle by which the rest of the *Terminator* franchise functions. *Terminator 2: Judgement Day* sends a second Arnold Schwarzenegger back in time to 1995 *as the good guy*, a reprogrammed T-800 robot sent by Future John Connor to save his ten year old self from a more sophisticated killer robot. They succeed, and manage to destroy the remaining components of the first movie's evil robot, thus setting back the production of (reverse-engineered) advanced computer processors and, they believe, averting Judgement Day altogether. When 1997 passed without a nuclear holocaust, it would have been verified that they changed the future's history. The catchphrase "No future but what we make," is uplifting from a humanist perspective, proving that we are masters of our own destinies.

Terminator 3: Rise of the Machines instead asserts that the most influential moments in history are predetermined, that their dates and events sequences are somewhat fluid, but that they are, eventually, inevitable. Judgement Day was unavoidable, the success of *T2* being to merely push the date back to July 24, 2004. This gives John more time to prepare, worried that the apocalypse was still coming, but it also gives the machines close to a decade of techno-logical advancement in their greatest weapon: Hollywood CGI. They send a leather-clad "Terminatrix" back with the primary mission of murdering the teenage versions of John Connor's future generals (as Connor himself dropped "off the grid" until he rose to power in the future human resistance), but with the overriding authority to murder Connor should his past self be detected, possibly trying to intervene in her plans. In killing some of these humans before being thwarted by Connor's band *on* Judgement Day, the timeline is significantly altered in favor of the machines *after*, John now without key mem-bers of his support staff.

Terminator: Salvation, contrary to its predecessors, occurs all in a single, linear time frame and involves no time travel at all, instead focusing on John Connor's attempts to battle the machines in 2018, when he has become something of a religious figure for seem-ing to know all about the future movements and innovations of the machine armies. John grapples both with convincing the remaining upper echelon military humans of his information, and with the

Girlpants and Gasoline

burden of trying to fulfill a prophesy older than himself. A prophesy which, in execution, looks like this:

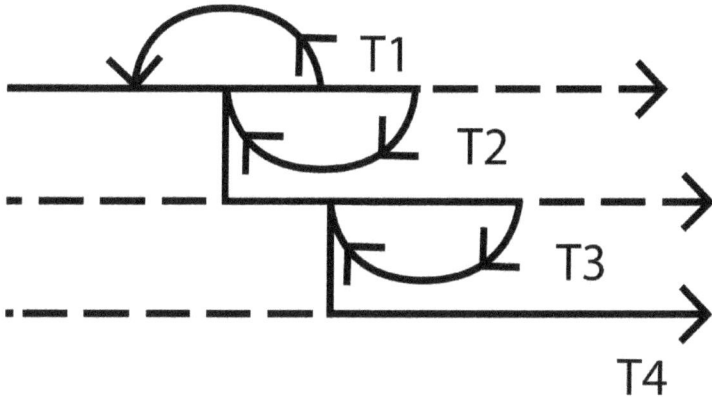

Figure 5. It's a lot like time travel sheet music.

Predetermination

Predeterministic time travel is the easiest to discuss, though it tends to lend itself only to the most humanly depressing world views. The case study is 2001's surrealist sci-fi teen tragedy *Donnie Darko*. Jake Gyllanhaal is the titular character Donnie, a boy with severe emotional issues and a history of mental illness. 'After' he begins sleepwalking, a jet engine crashes through his bedroom ceiling, certainly killing him had he not somnambulated out to a golf course that night. The engine appears to have literally fallen out of thin air. No planes having gone down, nor have they so much as flown over the town of Middlesex that night. Donnie manifests the ability to see "God's plan," liquid-like bubbles tubing out in front of people before they move and dictating their apparently predetermined actions. A hallucination that appears to be a man in a terrifying rabbit suit, named "Frank," warns Donnie that the world will end in just over 28 days. The bulk of the film then observes Donnie trying to tease out what makes a person 'good' or 'just,' and why a benevolent but suspiciously absent god would allow evil actions if, as it seems the case, free will is the illusory effect of not 'seeing' The Plan.

Predetermination casts God as something of an antagonist. All good and all evil, every choice in fact, is outside of human control and meted out in kind by a greater figure. There are no choices, and every action is a foregone matter. *Nothing* is actually good *or* evil, everything just is as it was always to have been. Any God figure becomes an antagonistic force because we *want* our choices to have meaning. Humans *want* to believe their choices can cause good or evil, otherwise any actions becomes meaningless or, even worse, excusable. No law can stand if breaking that law were 'God's will.' In Donnie's case, he mirrors this in his fruitless questioning of authority figures. Why do we act as if our actions will be judged by a personally involved deific figure? Why do we discourage the variety of human experience? Why does authority within any hierarchy seem to impress personal views downward and raise up hypocrisy? Why, actually, does any of this happen if no one has control?

The conclusion Donnie eventually accepts is that *everything* is predetermined, but the choices we make still matter *to us*. Yes, God controls him and everyone he knows, but *if no one notices, it's like we still have a choice*. 'Bad' things will happen, but there *is* a larger picture and at their ends every person is loved and no one is alone. It's terribly depressing as far as universal laws go, in a "What you don't know doesn't hurt you" sort of way, but it's also the reason time travel works in *Donnie Darko*. The 'Time Machine' is simply God, which nicely whitewashes any issues of power consumption or practical use. The explanation of How it works is actually a simple paradox: Donnie sees a hallucination which pulls him out of bed in the middle of the night, avoiding his getting crushed by a mysterious artifact that shouldn't be there. Donnie *should* have died, so when he does not it violates God's Plan, creating an alternate "tangent" universe. However, *nothing* can violate God's Plan, so the universe spirals in on itself and collapses back to the point at which it diverged from the original timeline. In doing so, the "temporal storm[4]" rips off a jet's engine and drops it on Donnie, who has accepted his role in the universe and God's Plan. The next morning, everyone and everything is fine, excepting Donnie, and no one has any memory of the movie's events because, from their perspective, nothing has happened. They have experienced a single, linear timeline, albeit with a weird relic from somewhen else dropping out of the sky. Donnie too, experienced a single flow of events, but to an outside observer (anyone watching the movie), the timeline looks quite a bit different.

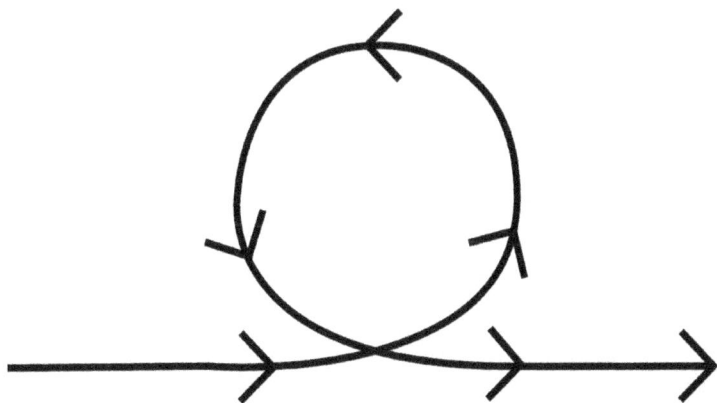

Figure 6. Please recycle your unused timelines.

This is a "God's eye view" of the movie. The running action leads up to Donnie violating God's plan, which causes a separate timeline that circles back on itself in a closed-loop, rejoining the original timeline. The problem with the paradox is how Donnie came to survive in the first place. Originally, he was lured out of bed by Frank, who we learn is killed and used by the Powers That Be specifically to guide Donnie back to his bed at the film's end in order to close the timeline. Similarly, the jet engine needs to come from the tangent universe 'before' the tangent universe gets created, and the only way for *that* to happen is if the tangent universe, created by violating God's Plan, were a *part* of God's Plan.

Multiple Realities

"Because God says so," seems like a pretty cheap cop-out, but in the film's context it's the expression of a solid, predetermined series of timelines not bound to a single universe. Multiversal theory considered, one may be *destined* to go against destiny. What is meant by "multiversal?" Imagine a timeline extending from the past, through the present, into the future. The past and the present are static, already decided facts, but the future can be represented as an infinite series of possibilities branching and intersecting from every point where a decision can be made, and the future altered. If we exist in a predeterministic universe, then these are the points at which events *will* happen that necessitate a resultant change somewhere else on the timeline. However, if existence *does* have even an inkling of free will in it, these are all *possible* futures, none of which are set in stone until events further transpire and certain possibilities are eliminated.[5] In this model, possible futures could exist *concurrently*.

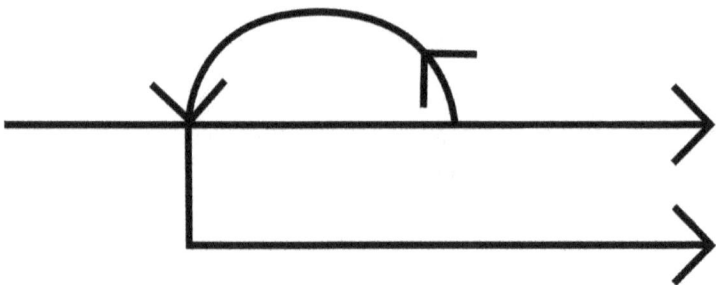

Girlpants and Gasoline

Figure 7. The "DBZ" model.

Here, two possible realities exist alongside each other, both stemming from a single event. Innately, every moment along a future timeline would bristle with divergent possible outcomes. *Figure 7* however depicts the Branch Event as resulting from a temporal journey. It is very similar to *Figure 4*, except the original timeline isn't necessarily overwritten by the shift in events. This is a very important distinction, because it allows for the possibilities that when you time travel, you:

a.   also travel between separate realities/universes within a "multiverse," and

b.   may return to either your original universe/time without having affected *it*, or the altered future of the 'new' universe, not knowing it to be different from your own and leaving the original timeline perhaps dangerously the same.

Though I'm loath to admit where the name comes from, out of some semblance of shame for not knowing any better at the time,[6] this is the "Dragon Ball Z" timeline model. Much of the show's fourth season deals with a character's future offspring coming back to save the hero's life so that the main characters stand a chance of surviving a future attack from terrible opponents. He aides the heroes in defeating these beings, but upon returning to the future finds that things are exactly as bad as when he left. He returns to face the next evil, helps kill *that one*, and then finally returns to his own future, where he uses his heightened abilities to finally eliminate both threats from *that* reality.

Internal Consistency

Time travel of any form, within a narrative, hinges on a

David E. Zucker

certain consistency. There's a distinction between it and "hard science fiction," such that even the silliest time stories can avoid plot holes, while more serious plots can get bogged down in trying to explain the physics of time travel with useless 'technobabble' that ends up discrediting itself. Take *Bill and Ted*, either one, really: major impediments to the boys' success are overcome simply by saying, '*After* we figure this out, we'll make sure to go back in time to set up a way for us to solve it *now*,' and then magically the solution reveals itself. It's ludicrous, but it follows the form of time travel set up by the rest of the movie: time flows in a preferred direction, so you must always dial *ahead* or risk coming out *before* you left, and since the future exists in order to come back in time and assist you with the simple existence of time traveling phone booth, so too is anything to *say* you are going to do set in stone, so long as you remember to get it done.[7] When Bill and Ted need Ted's dad's keys, Bill suggests they steal them. But the keys are already lost and there is no time to find them before their presentation is due, so the solution is to go do the presentation, and then when they have time, go back to when the keys *weren't* lost, steal them, and then leave them in a place to be found by the current Bill and Ted. Regardless of how they do on the presentation without their historical figures, afterward they still have a time machine, so even failing they can accomplish this task and assure that the 'next' iteration of Bill and Ted will be able to get their famous persons, get an A on the assignment, and then go back in time as successes to set up the loop again. From that point forward, the loop becomes a self-fulfilling prophesy of success. It may be convoluted to think about for anyone with an I.Q. over 90, but since Bill & Ted are simpletons they don't worry about the ramifications for destiny or forcibly 'fixing' the future before they get there. So long as they remember to do all the things they see happening as they go about their duties, the future is already set to favor them and ensure their success, even if it means the timeline is required by destiny to look like a crazy, crossing, squiggly yarn ball. And that's exactly

Girlpants and Gasoline

what it looks like when seen from inside the time booth. Ah, consistency.

Now is when I make myself sad. Flux capacitors and Mr. Fusions and self-fitting Nike's be damned, I can no longer find enjoyment in Michael J. Fox's chrono-hijinks because the movie doesn't follow a consistent internal logic.

Is Back to the Future a predetermined universe?

No. This is patently expressed by the notion that, when his future appears to be in doubt, Marty begins fading in and out of existence. If everything were predetermined, he would simply exist or not exist, based on the decision his young father makes to become assertive and win a girl's heart or not. More importantly, this shows that Marty has not simply entered a parallel universe's past where he cannot affect his own future. It could have been possible to say that when Marty changed the past he created a tangent universe completely separate from his own, i.e., the Dragon Ball scenario, and that returning to 'the' future meant only skipping forward to this new universe's corollary to his original place on the timeline. This would leave the original, miserable future intact, suddenly without a Marty and the new universe with two, which clearly isn't the case[8].

So Back to the Future is a divergent and over-written timeline?

Yes. The timeline Marty occupies can always be said to overwrite the one he came from, as events he becomes involved in have repercussions which alter his original present and future. By getting his parents together in a manner which makes George McFly to be an assertive, outgoing person in high school, when Marty returns to 1985 his family is financially well off with his father and siblings each having better jobs, his sister many boyfriends, and his mother is skinny and in a happy marriage. (Plus they all like his girlfriend and he has a boss truck.) Biff, the movie's asshole, is now a cowering beta male. However, as stated, Marty does not remember any of this in his past.

This is an incredible problem. That Marty's photograph of his siblings and then his own body begin fading from existence proves that anything and any person displaced from their own timeline is not completely cut off from the effects of causality they themselves precipitate. Since Marty did not immediately get written out of existence by disrupting his parents' original meeting, either his original timeline and his alteration of it are predestined, or there is still the chance that he could repair the damage and merely *alter* his timeline without destroying it. Since the process of fading exists in the first place, it is certain that Marty's universe is not predetermined, as a line, loop, or otherwise. Counter to this is the idea then, that Marty or his photo should fade *at all*. If they fade, then they are beholden to causality, and if Marty changes the timeline *he should be changed with it*. And yet he doesn't. Since upon 'returning' to his now-altered present Marty isn't immediately overwritten,[9] he seems to have escaped being completely affected by causality. His existence is contingent on not altering his past too much, but minor alterations only seem to affect people still in their native times, implying causality is itself localized to its own 'present' and becomes weaker when it has to echo backward through time. So the universe is 'semi-deterministic[10].'

But then in the next movie Marty and the Doc change the future and a newspaper from the following day changes immediately. An aged Biff steals the DeLorean and completely rewrites history, but the future timeline everyone else is in, and which Biff returns to, stays exactly as it is. Marty and the Doc do not get overwritten, but *both* have new-universe doppelgangers drastically different than themselves. Then they go back in time *again* and try to avoid running

Girlpants and Gasoline

into themselves. But in doing this, they end up making sure events turn out as they remember, when naturally they wouldn't! Doc hands himself the correct socket wrench when his previous self asks for the wrong one; Marty stalls Biff and his gang so that his father and their prior selves have the time to go through the events of the first movie as previously shown, implying they were there the whole time. So everything *has* to work out because it did, but nothing's predetermined and causality only applies when it makes the story more suspenseful.

Later, Marty goes back to the Hill Valley of the wild west to save 'his' version of the Doc who became stranded in time and died in the past. He takes a photo of the Doc's tombstone and this changes first to *Marty's* name, then disappears entirely when they both survive. They also save a schoolmarm from plummeting into a gorge, accidentally un-memorializing it back in 1985, ruin Biff's outlaw ancestor, and Marty undoes the crappy future he saw for himself and Jennifer in 2015, which she confirms with a disappearing fax message from said timeline. The Doc promises her that this is because "The future hasn't been written yet," which is very comforting in a "No future but what we make," sort of way, except that this of course happens at the foot of a now-wrecked DeLorean, including components from said future. So apparently there's no future but what we make, except the parts we've already been to and only for us, because that's now our past even if it'll never happen after it did.

Apparently "flux capacitor" is techie for "causal disruptor." Which would be great, if it wasn't also French for "childhood ruining magic bullshit box."

---

[1] The *original* cut, mind you.

[2] Pun not intended. Unless it was supposed to have been, in which case it always was going to be. We'll get into that later.

[3] Supposedly, a third movie is still in production, centered around the idea of a final time jaunt to help the boys write the one perfect song that brings the whole world

David E. Zucker

together, even though at the end of the last film they personally achieved peace in the Middle East, expended the world's nuclear arsenal fueling their stacks, filled the O-zone hole with air guitar, increased U.S. crop production, gave the Dow Jones its record high and played "Mars Stadium." Apparently that isn't good enough.

[4] I'm unabashedly stealing this term from an old *X-Men* cartoon episode involving Cable which, I'm sure, stole it from somewhere else. Probably a Jack Kirby era *Fantastic Four* piece. That guy sure liked storms of varying kinds and sizes.

[5] "Always in motion, the future is." - Yoda

[6] I still feel the need to explain this. When I was young there were only two Japanese cartoons on in the afternoon: *Dragon Ball Z* and *Sailor Moon*, and even then only about two seasons of each. Well after I grew out of watching these shows, I would be drawn back when I noticed the final episodes in rerun, hoping, always fruitlessly, that they would begin a new episode the following day. I think I was finally a teenager when, in the solitude of my room with no one to see my vice, I finally got to see how good triumphed over evil with ridiculously long-winded attack names. That said, I'll still sit and watch a "newish" episode if I channel surf past one.

[7] The converse is also true: Ted warns himself, "Remember to wind your watch," but since he apparently already forgot to do so, by the time his younger self *becomes* that Ted, he has of course forgotten and so reminds his younger self *again*, fulfilling the circular timeline. Since he is also something of an imbecile, he doesn't notice that this basically means he has no free will whatsoever.

[8] It is possible that this new universe's Doc ensured that Marty would be sent back in time to make sure his parents got together *exactly* as he remembered it, but this would require that multiple parallel Marty's traveling to the same time and place merge into a single being and not, you know, cause a universe-shattering paradox as described by Doc already. This however would never happen because it didn't *already* happen, and Marty has no memory of his supposedly now parallel life. They tried that in *The Butterfly Effect* and it was internally consistant, but still a shitty movie.

[9] Either by his own meddling or the meddling of *that* timeline's Marty, who would now have gone back in time and either merged with Marty-Prime and lost himself despite being the newer version or existing alongside his original. (Maybe he just ran off to live the sad life of an unnecessary clone. Like Ben Riley.)

[10] Given the same information and the same situation, a person can only choose the same response over and over, the single response the entirety of a life's experience would incline a person toward. The only way to do something *different* is to change the information (by experiencing the same thing previously in time and choosing differently in the future), or altering the past (either by explaining the outcome or affecting one's formative development possibly years prior, in order to instigate a different thought process and a different 'original' choice). In this regard, people really *are* akin to meat robots. Free will, then, is an illusion brought about by the paranoia of the human mind seeking to prove as fact the belief that it has any control over its own risk-reward analysis protocols. It could then be possible that while the universe is *not* predetermined in its entirety, without causal knowledge of (local) future events, people

Girlpants and Gasoline

would always 'choose' to behave in the way they are programmed, and any revision of timelines is due to the knowledge of future events and outcomes beating back this faux-predestination.

And since Marty doesn't possess *two sets* of memories, he has also gratefully avoided being Ashton Kutcher in *The Butterfly Effect*.

ABORTION, STAR TREK, AND THE INEVITABLE VICTORY OF REPRODUCTIVE RIGHTS

There are a surprising number of children conceived on or around active naval vessels within the *Star Trek* franchise. Off the top of my head I can recall:

- Captain Kirk's eldest illegitimate child, David ~~Shatner~~ Marcus
- The unborn child he conceived with a Native American ex-pat girl (who was then stoned to death) in that one episode where he lost his memory on a planet of other expatriated Native American humans
- Ian Andrew Troi (Deanna's hyper-gestated energy rape-baby on *Next Generation*)
- Mr. Worf's son, Alexander Rozhenko
- Miles O'Brien's second child, if not both
- Naomi Wildman on *Voyager*

Girlpants and Gasoline

- Captain Janeway's/Tom Paris' clutch of super-evolved lizard babies, but those can be discounted since even die-hard *Voyager* fans discount anything related to "Warp 10"
- Paris' and B'Elanna Torres' 1/4 Klingon daughter
- That time Trips (a man) got knocked up on *Enterprise*

A common thread amongst these? With the possible exception of Miles O'Brien's *first* child, his daughter, every pregnancy was a surprise,[1] often to both parents. Subtracting several cases of technical *rape* that go mostly glossed-over, ***if not overtly shamed or laughed-off by the crew***, we're left with three full-human and three partially-human children, all from species well known to be genetically compatible with humans. Let's remove Kirk's papoose because he had amnesia at the time. That still leaves David, born to Carol Marcus out of wedlock and raised *specifically* away from his father; Worf's son, born without his knowledge to the half-Klingon woman who rejected him almost immediately following consummation; O'Brien's second child, born to his wife while he was on active duty and therefor conceived on leave; Naomi Wildman, conceived without either parent's knowledge immediately before shipping out on what was supposed to be routine maneuvers; and Miral Paris, conceived again without specific intent while trapped in the Delta Quadrant (more of a surprise as Klingon-Human conception typically require some obstetrical tinkering).

By Roddenberry's ghost, you are telling me that by the 23rd–*even by the mid-24th*–century, mankind has not developed a 100% effective, simple method of birth control? We're at 99% now. We haven't closed that gap in almost three centuries? Worse, I am expected to believe that naval officers, *sailors on shore leave*, can't find a simple condom? Please. Tom Paris, with a reputation for being a ladies man and only 146 people to talk to for *seven years*, stranded in the Delta Quadrant, even after having his rationed replicator usage

David E. Zucker

reinstated couldn't replicate a simple pill? A hypospray? *A goddam sonic vasectomy readily available in 2014?* He was the Doctor's chief medic, for Cochrain's sake.

And the greatest Lothario of all the Terran people James Kirk doesn't use protection? *Really?* The man is very aware of his proclivity for promiscuity (barring bouts of mind control or amnesia). He's not a *moron*, he's a jackass. A player. If anyone were to be fastidious in his prevention of unintended or inconvenient pregnancies, would it not be the bedder of Orion slave girls? I'm sure penicillin comes in a handy photon bath, but babies are not a disease to be brushed aside. He would have taken precautions.

So there are two options to explain this phenomenon:

1. Abortion is strictly banned in either law or in practice within at least the confines of Starfleet, this likely reflecting at least a common trend if not written law within the greater human population, with close to no one considering it a viable option.
2. The choice of the mother to birth a child is paramount, except in extreme cases where the bearer's life is in danger. Abortion is not banned, and as a matter of choice supported as any other parental decision.

Deanna certainly becomes attached to her psychic light baby and refuses any medical treatment that might harm it, yet Troi's on-again/off-again Commander Riker suggests as much as terminating the invasive, unwanted pregnancy as the product of rape, firmly squashing the idea that in all forms abortion is either outlawed or carries anymore stigma than it does today. Similarly, B'Elanna Torres is offered a genetic procedure to correct her fetus' spinal deformity, but attempts further alteration to ensure the child does not outwardly express its Klingon phenotype. *This* is considered unethical by both her doctor and husband, but merits no disciplinary action. Demon-

Girlpants and Gasoline

strably, there are *some* ethical boundaries in regard to fetal life, but those lines are drawn at the cosmetic level. Conversely, Lieutenant Samantha Wildman chooses to birth and raise her mixed-race daughter alone, despite the father being a 75-year journey away and completely unaware of his progeny or that Wildman is still *alive*. Clearly, a mother's wishes seem to prevail over all others if there is no danger to her well being, but perhaps this is purely a *military* policy. Do the feelings of Earth civilians jive with those of Starfleet personnel?

It is Kirk of all people who describes the Federation's social conscience as a whole: Carol Marcus *chooses* to have her and Kirk's child, and *chooses* to raise David without any contact whatsoever from his father, and Kirk respects that, going so far as to be hated by the son he was never allowed to know, because that is what Carol's wished. Both parties accepted that a mother in a lab and a father captaining a starship on 5-year missions did not make a suitable family for a boy, but because Carol Marcus wished Kirk to remain completely uninvolved, Kirk acquiesced. Certainly he had some say in the matter as a free sentient, but Carol chose to raise her child and wished to do so alone, so Kirk did not fight her choice. An accidental pregnancy–despite advanced medical practices and free-energy in a post-monetary society–resulted from plain human irresponsibility and blind luck.[2]

Personal choice–personal *responsibility*–is what decides a life in *Star Trek*, a sentiment I imagine shared by many of its fans. That's always been the point, after all; that perhaps we're not ready–we are unsure–but we are here, we have come this far, and we are willing to *try*. That has always been the side of humanity Gene Roddenberry chose to believe in. The good, the uplifting, the willing to make an effort to succeed. *Star Trek* envisions a post-scarcity world, devoid of money and war, racial and religious bias. One world of many in a federated alliance, each with its unique customs and laws, each working together in the interest of exploration and discovery, peace without oppression. Freedom. Choice.

Star Trek is a Pro-Choice universe because it is at their very core noble and thematic of the human race to be granted the option of inflicting their will against each other, but choosing not to, to grant respect and autonomy to others not because it is easy, but the very opposite. We choose to have faith in the goodness of those around us, and, generally, we are rewarded. Some oppose even this freedom: despots, zealots, Klingons. They will demand that everyone else follow their words, their laws and decrees. And we let them make their demands because they too are entitled to it in our eyes. We may respond, we may ignore, we may even become oppressed at times, but ours is not a mutually exclusive freedom. It is a choice.

---

[1] Alright, I'm fairly sure Lizard-Paris and Lizard-Janeway were vaguely aware they were procreating but, again, "*Warp 10.*"

[2] This noticeably puts a darker spin on Kirk's actions during the run of *The Original Series*, knowing that somewhere he had a toddler he was "unsuitable" to even meet. That certainly explains displaced intimacy and commitment issues.

THE 10⁻¹² PERCENT: JEDI, ECO-NOMICS, AND THE HYPERELITE

Star Wars is one of those things nerds could–and *do*–argue about for hours. I'd be chief among them. You want to have one? Please do. I relish the opportunity, because instead of emotionally maturing as a child, I learned about *Star Wars*.

Part of the problem is that *Star Wars* became too big to be coherent decades ago. The expanded universe was fun, but with the release of prequels and now the promise of non-George-helmed sequels and a revised, singular continuity, there's a plethora of information that has to be wedged into old B-grade canon, much of which was frankly better and more sensical than the new films. Certain things get dropped by the wayside, however, and always have. Example: sentient beings tend to need to *buy* things with *money*.

Star Trek has always maintained that its Federation is a post-scarcity society. Cheap energy is made freely available as a public utility. Combined with replicator technology, functionally all necessities and luxury items can be created by anyone with enough free time and a minimum of effort. Careers exist more for the betterment of citizens and at their own discretion than on any real *need* for goods. Functionally, it is a socialist paradise. Only backward or tangential worlds, criminals, and the Ferengi maintain capitalist ideals.

Star Wars takes place in a galactic-scale capitalist culture. Banks have their own clans, Trade Federations start civil wars over tariff rates and embargo disputes. The capital of all known systems caters to the support of an upper-echelon elite, literally high up above the lower strata of Coruscant. In the Outer Rim, slavery is a common and accepted practice, especially on worlds controlled by the Hutts, an entire species primarily devoted to being crime lords.

Perhaps this has something to do with the level of technology achieved in each universe. *Star Trek* has faster-than-light travel, dematerializing transporters, and the ability to replicate anything from basic elemental building blocks, themselves saved as pure energy via the same mechanism as a transporter buffer. *Star Wars*, meanwhile achieves FTL transport, but transporters are relatively unknown and widely considered impossible (although short-range models have been demonstrably effective). Largely, however, means of production and distribution of goods remain in line with what we possess currently. Goods are produced either by hand or machine (sometimes both!) and curried from A to B by ship to be sold in stores for currency. Want a nice nerf steak and a cup of caf for a meal? Go to the ship's galley and heat up a couple, or make a reservation at your favorite eatery. Principles of technology may be more advanced, but the long-and-short of it is Aunt Beru had to go to market to buy her blue milk from a dairy farmer.

Herein lies a problem for the narrative: In *Star Wars* we rarely get to see what the average being is doing in the galaxy. Dictation and data pads are mentioned somewhat frequently, credits as a form of currency as well, and "(re)freshers" exist so that gentlefolks can

Girlpants and Gasoline

scrawl out an invoice or missive, buy a BlasTech DL-44 pistol, or take a sanisteam after a long hyperspace jaunt. Except that's boring, and as an audience, we tend to follow the action. If protagonists ever involve themselves in a financial transaction, it's either illicit, or a distraction. Consider primary characters:

- Jedi
- The Republic/Rebel Alliance/New Republic/Galactic Alliance/Galactic Federation of Free Planets (and associated militias)
- The Empire and
- Smugglers/non-affiliated outlaws

These are not the types to necessarily lament a lack of access to funds. Han Solo and his bands of rogues? They steal what they need, blast through security, and make a delivery to earn their payday. They've all won and lost fortunes a dozen times over–Lando Calrissian is famous for it. If a job didn't go bad, we wouldn't read about it. Federal governments don't exactly request expenditure reports during a war either. While the Rebels acquired their superior X-Wing fighters specifically through capture of the plans and defection of the creators, the Empire has entire worlds' resources at its disposal. It *is* an evil, tyrannical dictatorship, after all. At the top of society, the Skywalker-Solo clan owns multiple apartments, furnished many times over with expensive accoutrements and the highest, often illegal security measures. They are heroes among heroes. Leia was Galactic President, for god's sake. *Twice*. Three times, if you get technical. The sheer volumes of riches lavished upon them necessitated teams of specialized accountants just to manage. The result is that none of these characters ever need to worry about money for the rest of their lives, and–being appropriately paranoid for the eight most important beings in the galaxy–they have further access to hidden properties and assets. They don't even receive *spam mail.*

Even the Jedi are above the need for funding. Between all the money funneled into the organization through Luke and his friends, government subsidies and "gifts" of tactical armaments during times of crisis, the Jedi are perhaps the most well-trained, well-funded, and well-organized private army in existence, and yes I'm including the revived Mandalorian warriors. The Jedi maintain leagues of accountants whose sole purpose is to ensure that investments allow them to function completely autonomously from any governmental oversight. They go to the laundry and are handed a new robe from a Coruscanti employed by the Jedi Temple. They travel to Ilum to pick their own crystals to construct their own lightsabers.[1] Rather than living as ascetics, Jedi exist in a post-scarcity near-paradise *simply because they have more money than some star systems.*

As of 40 years post-Endor, there are approximately 400 known living Force users in the Jedi collective. Let us double that number to account for spouses and non-Force-sensitive family members who enjoy the perks of residing within this hyper-elite group. Let us now round off to an even *thousand* to compensate for the rotating cadre of bandits, allies, and planetary dignitaries who operate within those bubbles of influence. 1,000 beings who can circumvent, ignore, and otherwise flaunt the entire concept of a monetized economy and its legal system.[2]

Of the 100 *quadrillion* sentient beings estimated to be living in the Galaxy, the Jedi and their surrounding parties make up civilization's top 0.000000000001%.

They are The 10^{-12}%.

---

[1] If the costs of starship-grade antimater and fusable material weren't so expensive, one might almost consider this ceremony part of a green movement. [Insert Yoda pun.]

[2] The two Force users to be tried civilly on murder charges were sentenced to A)

Girlpants and Gasoline

temporary exile and research, which concluded after a year in which the Galactic Chief of State was ousted for treason, and B) a suspended death sentence under the custody of the successor to the man she murdered. Jedi are basically spoiled rich kids.

AN OPEN LETTER TO GEORGE LUCAS

My friend Carolyn has something of a point when she tells me my willingness to buy the complete Star Wars saga on Blu-Ray was kind of insane. It's the same movies I've seen literally hundreds and hundreds of times before. Yes, there were differences, though subtle and–at best–only truly appreciable if I'm willing to sit less than five feet from my television set (which of course I am).

If I may dig my own grave a bit deeper, this is in actuality the *sixth* version of the original trilogy I have owned and the *second* of the prequels:[1] The original version was taped off cable in the early-to-mid '80s on a single VHS tape, which I still have despite not owning a VHS player. The 1995 edition "digitally remastered by THX for sound" and the 1997 Special Edition boxed sets also sit idle on my shelf next to similarly sentimental tapes of *Teenage Mutant Ninja Turtles*, *SuperTed*, and *Robin Williams Live at the Met!* Somewhat more functionally, I own the original release DVDs of all the prequels and 2004 release of the Original Trilogy with once again

Girlpants and Gasoline

cleaned up additions, then the *2006* editions which included the (sigh...fullscreen) original and *unaltered* Trilogy. Then the Blu-Ray boxed set. Oh, yes, and I owned the complete 1995 edition on *Laserdisc* for a number of years until I humiliatingly lost them to Kevin Smith's Secret Stash in a televised test of my nerdistry.[2]

And I *still* bought the boxed set. Hell, there wasn't ever any question. It was available for pre-order less than a day when I forked over my credit card. The only question—the one all fans continue to ask themselves—is this:

"Why do I still give George Lucas my money?"

He keeps screwing with my favorite things. Every new home video release alters in some way the movies I had long since committed to photostatic memory. Graciously, at this point most of the edits seem to be correcting previous errors, either initial or subsequent upon previous additions. Luke's blade is blue again, or a 1970s special effect cut is smoothed out. Han even shoots not-first-but-almost-kind-of-concurrently-with Greedo, now. Yeah, Darth Vader says "NOOOoooo!" again, and Ewoks now blink, which is somehow far creepier than the adorable, always-staring, ever-moist Henson masks used to be, but at this point everything's cosmetic. They're not reinserting the lost "Sandstorm" scene, though that I might be okay with.

Truthfully, I've long gotten over the idea that George Lucas refuses to tell me the same story twice, even if I'm going to pay for it nine times. He catches a lot of flack for it, but I've always thought of him as 'Uncle George.' Uncle George used to bear us on his back and play "horsey." We'd ride around and make Tauntaun sounds and fall down laughing, inventing wild stories and saving the galaxy.

One day Uncle George had to tell us we were getting too big to play horsey anymore. He just couldn't lift us. It's wasn't a maturity thing, he'd still play with us, but the games would have to change.

David E. Zucker

We had been changing all this time and finally it was just too much weight to put on his shoulders. We had to cary ourselves from then on.

Yes, we were disappointed, but we understood. We smiled and played chess, and we talked with Uncle George about trade embargoes and tariff law, congressional procedure. Then one day we caught Uncle George playing horsey with our sister's kids and saving the galaxy and we resented the man. We resented him so much. How *dare* he? This was *our* game. He created it, but *we* owned it together. We were as much a part of the experience as he was, we were the audience, the only audience. We had been raised on it. It was canon law. How dare he sully that history by reinventing and repurposing our childhood happiness for others?

Because it's *his* game. He can do whatever he wants with it and I just have the sit back and take it with maturity because *I'm a big boy now. Star Wars* isn't about maturity. It never has been. It's been about magic and fairy tales and the hero's journey in the most culturally prolific and dominant story-telling form of the last forty years. The fall of the prequels was one thing, it was trying to fill a backstory and flesh out an entire galactic civilization while simultaneously retaining puppets for the children. It was off, but not because it wasn't *Star Wars*.

We are no longer Uncle George's target audience.

We cannot be mad he can still play children's games with his new children. Hell, we raised these kids. We should be proud that Grandpa George is still around to teach our kids what it means to be a Jedi and let the Force guide you in your heart. The game doesn't end just because we are too old to play it, it just means we have to take on a different role if we want to keep playing.

As a fanbase, we need to accept that the artistic work was obscured for us long ago. We can all shadow-cast *The Empire Strikes*

Girlpants and Gasoline

Back like "Rocky Horror" at this point. We know the story; we know the finer points of galactic representative democracy, political theater. Watching Senator Palpatine is for us like watching Rob Lowe and the mom from "Weeds" in old episodes of "The West Wing." We watch *Star Wars* with so much back story and extraneous running commentary in our heads that the cinematic experience, even the artistic product is clouded. None of us could ever watch *Star Wars* again like it was any other movie.

Why would I want to? *Star Wars* is everything wonderful about my childhood, untainted by any of the memories of what childhood was actually like. I don't remember Y2K terror, I remember 4 days of freezing, torrential rain at the very first official Star Wars Celebration outside of Denver in May of 1999 and being thankful for just being there. Being outside the target demographic just means that I can afford to buy all the coolest, most expensive toys I didn't have as a kid. It means if I want to be a Jedi, I can sew my own costume. It means sitting down in a cantina, sipping on good whiskey, and asking the cute girl at the end of the bar if she's from the moons of Iego, because she must be an angel.

The game doesn't end just because we are too old to play it, it just means we take on different rolls to keep playing.

---

[1] Not including the *Phantom Menace* VHS I owned because DVDs weren't very prominent in 2000. I also later bought both the widescreen *and* fullscreen DVDs of *Episode II*, because DVDs still came either-or at the time.
[2] Oh, and I burned a fan-edit of *Episode IV* with better effects to disc and printed out its custom slipcase insert. But that's it, I swear.

THAT TIME I ACCIDENTALLY INTERVIEWED JOHN POPPER OF BLUES TRAVELER

My junior year of college I chose to fulfill my Brit Lit I. assignment in an 8:30 a.m., thirty-person class proctored directly by the professor, instead of the 200-something class later in the day, where I would only be beholden to a mild T.A. and attendance. The reason for this was expressed concisely on Day 1 when the professor asked us to write down, among other things, what we hoped to gain out of this class: "To endear myself to you enough that, should I have to petition to get into your Comics class next semester, you'll let me[1]."

In any event, this class was engaging and amusing, and allowed a bit more ... creativity with our projects than I imagine the larger class was given. One of which I was specifically looking forward to was–to illustrate how much of a nerd I was–to compare any modern musical number to the poetry we had been reading.

Girlpants and Gasoline

While I'm sure some students would have done well to compare Surrey and Rochester to "Bump 'n Grind," I was determined to find a modern pop/rock classic that followed perfectly a Shakespearean sonnet. It was a short assignment, devoid of any mission or attempt to describe the larger world, merely an order to be descriptive and convincing enough as to show our understanding of absorbed material. What follows, to illustrate a point, is that resultant paper minus copyrighted material:

When I first sought a song written in the form of a sonnet, I began with my favorite music and songs that had recently caught my ear. Sadly, it turned out that all of my preferred music was based on syncopated, unrhymed lyrics. After three days of analyzing everything I could, I threw in the towel on my way to class and queued up some just generally fun music for my own enjoyment–a playlist where every song is based off of the chord progression from Pachelbel's Canon in D. Three steps out the door I was struck by the musical equivalent of Shakespeare's Sonnet 55: "Hook," by Blues Traveler. By form, it is comprised almost entirely of sonnets; by rhyme, it covers multiple sonnet forms; by theme it is Shakespearean. This is why John Popper sings that the "hook" of the song is what pulls a listener back in.

The English Sonnet is often referred to as the Shakespearean sonnet, not just because Shakespeare became the most prolific poet to have utilized the form, but also in that, while earlier English poets had mostly translated and built off Italian originals, Shakespeare was truly innovative in his use of the sonnet, breaking traditions and striving to create something new. Of the several rhyme schemes used in English Sonnets, Shakespeare favored the format of three quatrains rhyming a-b-a-b, c-d-c-d, and e-f-e-f, followed by a rhyming couplet, g-g. This is the exact pattern by which "Hook" opens. Taken in blocks, the first verse-and-chorus and the second verse-and-chorus

David E. Zucker

are rhymed in this very precise manner.

However, as any drunken undergrad in front of a beer pong table, angrily shouting for someone to put on Four can tell you, "Hook" is most memorable for its ludicrously fast second half. While this section does not fit into the form of a Shakespearean sonnet, taking the time to space out the lines by rhyme and rhythm reveals something both fascinating and amusing to the educated listener:

Just as the sonnet has multiple rhyme schemes, so does "Hook." Throughout what could be called the 'breakdown' in "Hook," one finds the major sonnet rhyme schemes of a-b-a-b, a-b-b-a, and even a-a-a-a, as well as multiple couplets.

Why would Blues Traveler make such a break from the Shakespearean sonnet form? For this, one must examine the lyrical and thematic content of both "Hook" and Sonnet 55. Shakespeare's Sonnets, as stated, were made famous not just because he himself became famous, but because they were vastly more innovative than what what had come before. Originally, English Sonnets were merely translations of Italian Sonnets, expressly the Petrarchan Sonnets. 'Original' English works up until Shakespeare's time followed along with the major goal of the Renaissance, that is, to mirror Classical works.

In light of this, early English sonnets were flowery and full of classical imagery, likening lovers unto famous figures and generally producing the 17th Century equivalent of that which is currently read by nineteen year olds in itchy sweaters and horn-rimmed glasses, as they strum sadly on their guitars in Starbuckses across the country.

What Shakespeare did with the sonnet I can only describe as "ballsy," taking the form as-is while professing his own works and subjects to build off classical models and actually surpass them. In Sonnet 55 Shakespeare describes "the gilded monuments of princes," marble, statues and edifices as being great, yes, but bound to the death and decay of time. Invoking the classical figure, Shakespeare claims even Mars' sword and the fires of war will not destroy this sonnet. As Shakespeare says, his lover shall live eternally in the poem, and the poem itself shall last until the very end of time at Judgement Day. To reject the accepted model for an art is one matter, but to openly use it to compare itself poorly with your own work is a powerful statement, and it takes great talent to defend. This is in fact the message in "Hook." As Popper sings in the opening stanza, what he says doesn't matter, so long as he instills in the audience a specific feeling, and in fact his very job is to force this state of being upon listeners whether or not they desire this particular effect.

The verse comprises the first two stanzas of the opening 'sonnet,' while the subsequent chorus completes a couplet. These lines expressly state that it is the job of the singer (John Popper) to say something, but what that something is doesn't particularly matter as it is the hook of a song–the catchy, repetitive musical bit–that will draw listeners back in.

Furthering their rejection of musical tradition, Blues Traveler invokes in the second "sonnet" the literary opposite of "Hook," and of course say they are doing exactly that. After explaining that they will reference great heroes in order to muddy their true purposes, they do exactly that, referencing Peter Pan and amusing us with a pun on the word/name "Hook." It's merely a tactic by which to obscure the superfluous nature of everything beyond the musical hook, and they make no attempt to actually hide this because your resistance is irrelevant. They have already caught you.

Interestingly, this same play on words reinterprets their hero in a cowardly light. Peter Pan could face the personification of growing old and cynical, his Hook, but he could not admit these realities and so retreated back into his Neverland, much as the song implies the hook reels in its audience.

Running into the breakdown section, Blues Traveler cements its position against the music of convention. Popper demands the listener, everyone from Rin Tin Tin and Anne Boleyn, ingest the song and understand it, to see what empty copies of the same song over and over do to a truly creative person, the singer and the artist.

The singer condemns MTV and political correctness, willing to sing of love so long as he can sing of "rage and hate and pain and fear of self" as well, the entire human condition. The singer says he has tried to keep silent but that he no longer can, and though it might be his financial ruin as a popular musician, he must refuse to write for merely the purpose of commercial success through being "catchy" and "hip."

Popper laments that he may in fact be kidding, and that his tirade was at worst a rant, and at best a prayer to the tastes of his audience. Ultimately, when Popper is down-and-out and need a quick influx of cash, it's not artistic expression of even luck that he'll turn to, but the hook. While Blues Traveler might be better than mere utilizers of the hook and convention, they still depend on these features for the foundations of their livelihood.

Many mornings, I wake up with a song stuck in my head. Usually it's something I recently listened to, but sometimes not. Often, it's "Hook." Maybe it's because the breakdown is the same tempo as my alarm, maybe the bird outside my window is the same pitch, but my brain takes that and turns it into John Popper's voice. That's catchy. That's a hook.

I like "Hook" because of the rhyme scheme. I like it because of the enjambment–now that I know the word for it–in the break-down–and I like the anti-pop mentality, but I wake up singing songs like this because of the hook. By rhyme, theme, and form "Hook" is the 20th Century descendant of Shakespeare's more self-touting sonnets, namely Sonnet 55. Matching modern lyrics for bounce and innovation, perhaps this explains the morning where half asleep I find myself reciting "To be, or not to be" over and over in the shower. Shakespeare has his own hooks.

Girlpants and Gasoline

This comparison would be entirely irrelevant after my completion of the aforementioned English course if not an offhanded comment by my friend Dean years later: while listening to "The Hook" in his car, I idly mentioned that I had once written a paper on the song. He suggested I post said paper as a daily blog post the next time I couldn't think of anything to write. Taking his advise, I queued it up to run on the night of my birthday, when I would be sure to have more immediately drunk concerns. After reading it a few days later, and being "All about Twitter," he eagerly suggested I tweet the whole thing to Blues Traveler. What the hell, right? I didn't even know Blues Traveler had its own Twitter handle but, sure enough, John Popper and co. can be addressed at @Blues_Traveler[2].

As it turns out, John Popper actually checks and maintains that account and replies from it. He also apparently–as of November 2011–tweets like my father texts. That is to say overly verbose and with odd, culturally muddled abbreviations. Over the course of ten reply tweets, Popper @-ed me the following:

"Wow... I did not know alot of that!... Intuition led alot of my feel for respecting&rejecting traditional form intermitently | but my desiration of Pachebel was my first aim. Actually the song was built on the premise of my older brother mentioning | that I use too many words in a verse... So my aim was to do the first two verses

"normal",&cram way too many into the "3rd" | verse(which became the break down)... But the subdivision of rhyme scan into rhyme within a "rhyme" while not perhaps | Shakespear's brand of gin,is a practice as old as the hills... Especially with lymrics or iembic scans...actually rap does | it alot... But I'd wager most devises have been effected by the Bard...&certainly his ability to take what had come before& | innovate is a trademark of every innovater I aspire to...Bob Marley didn't do alot of the "reggae" things we now associate | with a genre we give him credit for inventing. Likewise Hendrix broke many of his own rules of the new guitar style he | himself was establishing... I expect no less from arguably the greatest master of the english language ever..

David E. Zucker

But I was | really impressed with that report&must now track down
sonnet#55... Thanx for that... ;)" [sic.]

Let's set aside the spelling and grammatical errors for a
moment. There's no doubt John Popper is a lyrical madman, but
typist may not be on his resume and he had to fit all of that into 140
character chunks[3].

The reason, the only reason, any of this is important, is that
you can sit down and discern exactly why a thing is great, why it's
culturally important and honest, why it matters beyond the confines
of how it was originally packaged. You can draw similarities and
parallels to the greatest works of mankind and convince even its
original creator that it follows in a long line of magnificence. You can
do all that and it may still just turn out to be the case that someone
was trying to annoy the piss out of his older brother.

Does it take anything away from the work, to know that its
meaning is not intentionally manifold and complex? Is it somehow
less great for being accidentally so? Or does this grant the artistic
product a more miraculous quality? That such artistic beauty and
rhythm could be achieved unintentionally or at least without conscious intellectual thought, doesn't that convey both a simple earnestness and a latent quality of quiet genius buried deep in its DNA? Or
is it simply the case that we invent meaning in a work irrespective of
authorial intent? That when we like something, we must make it
great to justify our liking it? Must it be complex and layered and
subversive to be worthwhile? And if so, why can't we accept an
honest and simple pursuit as it is for what it is?

We live in an age where nothing is what it seems, unless it's
only doing so ironically. We come to expect the unexpected as a
performance art. Every man is a one-man show. Every act exactly
that. Earnestness is, quite frankly, unexpected, confusing, and often-
times downright alarming.

---

[1] A point of order: though I was able to register without having to petition, I believe I completely succeeded in my primary goal, likely on the day I convinced my work group to cast our version of *Sir Gawain and the Green Knight* as an animated feature, starring Judd Nelson in the titular role and a cameo by Sir Patrick Stewart as Arthur.

[2] Incidentally, typing and saying "at" before the @ symbol is linguistically appalling. We should really find a better solution to this.

[3] Alright, "affect/effect" and "alot/a lot," "iembic" and "innovater" and "lymric" and "Shakespear" are problematic, but, again, *INTERNET*. Moving on.

Proof I Am Not A Liar

Events in this book have been recorded faithfully, to the best of my recollection, and involved parties have been consulted when necessary. Certain names may have been changed to protect the innocent, but weren't. No one is innocent.

Certain quotations of professionals have been sourced from public forums for purposes of transparency:

The Death Throes of Print Media
Josh Lesnick on digital watches:
https://twitter.com/superhappy/status/1472127075
https://twitter.com/superhappy/status/1472130052
Randal K. Milholland on T-shirts:
https://twitter.com/choochoobear/status/1509336283
On cavemen:
https://twitter.com/choochoobear/status/1509377078

Girlpants and Gasoline

Ryan North on newspapers:
http://qwantz.livejournal.com/107040.html

That Time I Accidentally Interviewed John Popper of Blues Traveler
https://twitter.com/blues_traveler/status/134916311749894144
https://twitter.com/blues_traveler/status/134916812776275968
https://twitter.com/blues_traveler/status/134917132717797376
https://twitter.com/blues_traveler/status/134917604916736001
https://twitter.com/blues_traveler/status/134918089404985347
https://twitter.com/blues_traveler/status/134918415809916928
https://twitter.com/blues_traveler/status/134918921408090112
https://twitter.com/blues_traveler/status/134919299696562176
https://twitter.com/blues_traveler/status/134919631205974016
https://twitter.com/blues_traveler/status/134919868804902912

An Open Letter to Gorge Lucas
http://www.imdb.com/title/tt2505482/

Acknowledgements

So many people need to be thanked for contributing in bizarre fashions to this book that, like an Oscar-winning actor, I am liable to forget many obvious individuals. Rather than attempt and fail, I hereby nominate certain people to accept their thanks on behalf of countless others.

To Mrs. Diane Travis, the first teacher willing to tell me I was good enough to write professionally, and lie to me saying I could make a living off it. Thank you.

To Dr. Ryan Vaughan, D.F.A., who got his doctorate in comedy and still laughed at my jokes anyway, many of which have been recycled into this very book. Thank you for letting, encouraging, and even assigning me to write serious, scholarly papers about Pauly Shore and Jersey Shore and the fat kid from Drake and Josh.

Girlpants and Gasoline

To the weird, slightly lecherous professor who taught my Intro to Crit class who kind of looked like Duncan MacLeod from Highlander: your class was terrible, but everything we read after Marx was fascinating. I would have no conception of proper feminist, Orientalist, or postmodernist theories if not for the reading we did. To a greater extent in this field, I would also like to thank the website and blogging platform Tumblr for teaching me gender equality better than Barthes.

To Carolyn Ann De Melo, for more than I could properly thank in a lifetime.

For my friends, I ask the credit be shared between Dean McGowan, my longest friend; Mike Kesselman and Matt Mutino, the two most willing to indulge hour-long debates on the intricacies of subcultural linguists and terminology or the Dewey decimal system; and Jay O'Neill, who seems the least credible but is most assuredly real. I still maintain that we are not human beings, but for the most part very well-written characters.

As for my family, I thank you for giving me both the stories I tell and the genetic/experiential lottery allowing me the foresight to write them all down. I trust you'll deny most of the good ones.

Lastly, and oddly, I'd like to thank author Chuck Klosterman. We met only once, very briefly at a book signing, and I could think of nothing I considered genuine or interesting to say so I only asked you to sign my favorite of your books, but you are definitively the reason this book exists. Your works showed me that pop-culture journalism was a thing, that Gonzo hadn't disappeared, and most importantly (and this is entirely egotistical and backwards on my part) that success was possible for someone who wrote like me. Also, all the footnotes? Yeah, those are all your wonderful fault.